GENKI

AN INTEGRATED COURSE IN ELEMENTARY JAPANESE
THIRD EDITION

初級日本語［げんき］

げんき I

〔第3版〕

ワークブック
WORKBOOK

坂野永理・池田庸子・大野裕・品川恭子・渡嘉敷恭子
Eri Banno / Yoko Ikeda / Yutaka Ohno / Chikako Shinagawa / Kyoko Tokashiki

D1231414

the japan times PUBLISHING

初級日本語 げんき I ［ワークブック］
GENKI: An Integrated Course in Elementary Japanese I [Workbook]

2000 年 2 月 20 日　初版発行
2011 年 3 月 20 日　第 2 版発行
2020 年 3 月 5 日　第 3 版発行
2022 年 2 月 20 日　第 15 刷発行

著　者：坂野永理・池田庸子・大野裕・品川恭子・渡嘉敷恭子
発行者：伊藤秀樹
発行所：株式会社 ジャパンタイムズ出版
　　　　〒 102-0082 東京都千代田区一番町 2-2　一番町第二 TG ビル 2F
　　　　電話 (050)3646-9500 （出版営業部）
ISBN978-4-7890-1731-2
本書の無断複製は著作権法上の例外を除き禁じられています。

First edition: February 2000
Second edition: March 2011
Third edition: March 2020
15th printing: February 2022

Illustrations: Noriko Udagawa
English translations and copyreading: Umes Corp. and Jon McGovern
Narrators: Miho Nagahori, Kosuke Katayama, Toshitada Kitagawa, Miharu Muto, and Rachel Walzer
Recordings: The English Language Education Council, Inc.
Typesetting: guild
Cover art and editorial design: Nakayama Design Office (Gin-o Nakayama and Akihito Kaneko)
Printing: Nikkei Printing Inc.

Published by The Japan Times Publishing, Ltd.
2F Ichibancho Daini TG Bldg., 2-2 Ichibancho, Chiyoda-ku, Tokyo 102-0082, Japan
Phone: 050-3646-9500

Website: https://jtpublishing.co.jp/
Genki-Online: https://genki3.japantimes.co.jp/

ISBN978-4-7890-1731-2

Printed in Japan

本書について

　このワークブックはテキスト『初級日本語 げんき』の補助教材です。今回『げんき』第3版を制作するにあたり、テキストの改訂内容に合わせてワークブックも加筆修正を行いました。

　「会話・文法編」には、第1課の前にひらがな練習カード、第2課の前にカタカナ練習カードがあります。まずは文字を学んでから、練習に取り組んでください。各課には、テキストで導入された各文法項目につき1ページのワークシートがあります。ワークシートでは既習の文法項目や語彙も復習しながら学習項目の定着を図ることができます。対応する文法項目の番号が表示されているので、必要に応じてテキストの文法説明を確認してワークブックに取り組むといいでしょう。

　各文法項目を学習した後は、「答えましょう」と「聞く練習」で総合的な練習を行うことができます。「聞く練習」には1課につき、会話文を中心として3つまたは4つの問題が収録してあります。

　「読み書き編」は、漢字の練習シート（Kanji Practice）と漢字の穴埋め問題（Using Kanji）で構成されています。『げんきⅠ』のワークブックには英文和訳もあります。漢字の導入後、書き方を覚えるまで、この漢字練習シートを使って何度も書いてみましょう。まず、漢字のバランスを意識して薄く書かれている文字をなぞってから、右側の空欄に何度も書いて練習します。筆順はテキストの漢字表を参考にしてください。

　穴埋め問題は、文の中に漢字や熟語が意味のあるものとして含まれていますから、必ず文全体を読んでから解答してください。『げんきⅠ』の英文和訳の練習では、習った漢字をできるだけ使って文を書いてみましょう。

　このワークブックをテキストと併用することで、より効率よく初級日本語を学ぶことができるでしょう。

About This Book

This workbook is designed as a supplement for the textbook *GENKI: An Integrated Course in Elementary Japanese*. The production of the textbook's third edition has required additions and other changes to the workbook to bring it into conformity with the new text.

The Conversation and Grammar section in this book provides *hiragana* practice cards before Lesson 1, and *katakana* practice cards before Lesson 2. Before you begin doing the exercises, be sure to learn these characters. Every lesson contains a worksheet for each grammar point introduced in the textbook. In addition to providing practice on new material, the worksheets also help you to reinforce your understanding of grammatical topics and vocabulary encountered in earlier lessons. The serial number of each grammar point is listed so that you can, if necessary, quickly look up the relevant explanation in the textbook and review it before doing the workbook practice.

After studying each new grammatical idea, you are given the opportunity to review the material comprehensively through the Questions and Listening Comprehension sections. The Listening Comprehension section for each lesson features three or four tasks that involve listening to dialogues and other recorded material.

The Reading and Writing section consists of kanji worksheets (Kanji Practice) and fill-in-the-blank questions about the kanji (Using Kanji). Volume 1 also includes English-to-Japanese translations. Newly introduced kanji should be written over and over on the sheet until memorized. First, trace the lightly printed kanji samples, paying attention to the balance of the characters. Then practice by copying the kanji over and over again in the blank spaces to the right. For stroke order, please refer to the kanji chart in the textbook.

For the fill-in-the-blank questions, you should read the entire sentence before filling in the blanks in order to learn kanji in context. When practicing the English-to-Japanese translations in Volume 1, you should use previously studied kanji whenever possible.

By using this workbook in tandem with the textbook, you will learn elementary Japanese with greater efficiency.

げんき① ワークブック　もくじ

読み書き編
_{よ か へん}

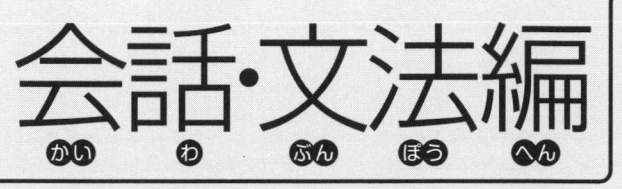

会話・文法編
かい　わ　ぶん　ぽう　へん

Conversation and Grammar

Japanese Writing System —1 *Hiragana* 🔊 W-JWS1

1. Listen to the audio and study the *hiragana* characters.
2. When you have familiarized yourself with the characters, cut out the cards along the solid lines and practice reading each *hiragana*, and check against the romanization on the back.

	a	*i*	*u*	*e*	*o*
	あ	い	う	え	お
k	か	き	く	け	こ
s	さ	し	す	せ	そ
t	た	ち	つ	て	と
n	な	に	ぬ	ね	の
h	は	ひ	ふ	へ	ほ
m	ま	み	む	め	も
y	や		ゆ		よ
r	ら	り	る	れ	ろ
w	わ				を
	ん				

o	e	u	i	a
ko	ke	ku	ki	ka
so	se	su	shi	sa
to	te	tsu	chi	ta
no	ne	nu	ni	na
ho	he	fu	hi	ha
mo	me	mu	mi	ma
yo		yu		ya
ro	re	ru	ri	ra
o (wo)				wa
				n

あいさつ　Greetings

➤ What are these people saying? Write in Japanese (*hiragana*) the appropriate expression for each situation.

1. おはじよう

2. ありがとう

3. こんばんは

4. すみません

5. いただきます

6. ごちそうさま

7. いってきます
8. いってらっしゃい

9. ただいま
10. おかえり

11. はじめまして

12. さいようなら

13. おやすみ

14. こんにちは

すうじ　Numbers

➤ Read or listen to the following numbers and write them in Arabic numerals. 🔊 W-Suuji

(a) ご　　　5

(b) ぜろ　　0

(c) きゅう　9

(d) さん　　3

(e) なな　　7

(f) に　　　2

(g) ろく　　6

(h) いち　　1

(i) はち　　8

(j) よん　　4

(k) じゅうろく　　16

(l) よんじゅう　　40

(m) にじゅういち　　21

(n) ひゃくろくじゅうよん　　164

(o) きゅうじゅうに　　92

(p) さんじゅうご　　35

(q) ななじゅうろく　　76

(r) じゅうはち　　18

(s) ひゃくごじゅうなな　　157

(t) ひゃくいち　　101

クラス [   ]
(Class)

なまえ [   ]
(Name)

第1課 1 X は Y です

だい いっ か

☛ Grammar 1

I Look at Takeshi's profile and describe him in Japanese.

1. たけしさんは <u>にじゅうにさい です</u> 。

2. たけしさんは <u>にほんじん です</u> 。

3. たけしさんは <u>よねんせい</u> 。

Takeshi, 22 years old
Japanese
4th-year student

II Using the framework "X は Y です," translate the following sentences into Japanese.

1. Ms. Ogawa is Japanese.

<u>おがわさん</u> は <u>にほんじん</u> です。

2. Mr. Takeda is a teacher.

たけださんは せんせい です。

3. I am an international student.

わたしは りゅうがくせい です。

4. Haruna is a first-year student.

はるなは いちねんせい です。

5. Ms. Yamamoto is 25 years old.

やまもとさんは にじゅうごさい です。

第1課 だい いっ か 2 Question Sentences   ☛Grammar 2

Ⅰ Look at the chart on p. 46 of the textbook and complete the conversation.

1. Q：メアリーさんは_____
    め あ り い   *1st-year student?*

   A：いいえ、にねんせいです。

2. Q：やましたせんせいは_____
                              how old?

   A：よんじゅうななさいです。

3. Q：たけしさんは_____
                              Japanese?

   A：_____

4. Q：ロバートさんは_____
    ろ ば あ と   *what year (in school)?*

   A：_____

Ⅱ Ask the right questions in each of the following exchanges.

1. A：_____

   B：よねんせいです。

2. A：_____

   B：じゅうきゅうさいです。

第1課 だい いっ か　3　Noun₁ の Noun₂

☞Grammar 3

Ⅰ Translate the following phrases into Japanese using the framework "A の B." Note that the order in which the two nouns appear may be different in English and in Japanese. Read Grammar 3 (p. 43).

1. Takeshi's telephone number

   たけしのでんわばんごう

2. my friend

   わたしの ともだち

3. Japanese-language teacher

   にほんごの せんせい

4. Yui's major

   ゆいさんの せんこう

5. high school teacher

   こうこうの せんせい

Ⅱ Translate the following sentences into Japanese.

1. My major is Japanese language.

2. I am a student at Nihon University.

3. Professor Yamashita is a Japanese language teacher.

4. Is Takeshi a student at Sakura University?

   Yes, that's right.

第1課　4　Time and Telephone Numbers
だい いっ か

Ⅰ Time—Look at the following pictures and write the answers.

1.　**05:00** PM

Q：いま　なんじですか。
A：ごじ ごじ です。

2.　**09:00** AM

Q：いま　なんじですか。
A：ごぜんくじ です。

3.　**12:30** PM

Q：いま　なんじですか。
A：ごご じゅうにじ はんです。

4.　**04:30** AM

Q：いま　なんじですか。
A：ごぜんしじ はん です。

Ⅱ Telephone Numbers—Ask three people what their phone numbers are and write down the numbers in both Japanese and Arabic numerals.

1. _____

(Arabic numerals:)

2. _____

(Arabic numerals:)

3. _____

(Arabic numerals:)

第1課　5　こたえましょう (Questions)
だい いっ か

▶ Answer the following questions in Japanese.

1. おなまえは？

2. おしごと (occupation) は？

3. なんねんせいですか。

4. なんさいですか。

5. せんこうは なんですか。

6. でんわばんごうは なんばんですか。

第1課　6　きくれんしゅう (Listening Comprehension)
だい いっ か

A Listen to the phrases and choose the correct picture from below. 🔊 W01-A

1. (　　　)　2. (　　　)　3. (　　　)　4. (　　　)　5. (　　　)　6. (　　　)

7. (　　　)　8. (　　　)　9. (　　　)　10. (　　　)　11. (　　　)

(a)　(b) 　(c)

(d) 　(e) 　(f)

(g) 　(h) 　(i)

(j)　(k)

B Listen to the dialogues between a passenger and a flight attendant in an airplane. Find out the times of the following cities. 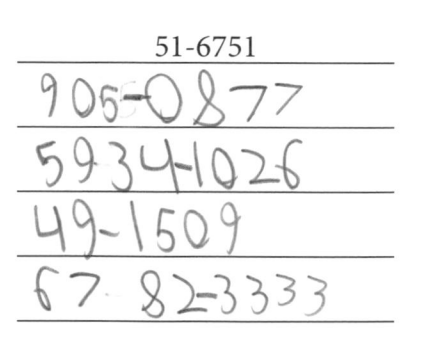 W01-B

(Example) とうきょう	8:00 A.M.
1. パリ (Paris)	4:00 A.M.
2. ソウル (Seoul)	9:00 P.M.
3. ニューヨーク (New York)	1:00 P.M.
4. ロンドン (London)	7:30 A.M.
5. タイペイ (Taipei)	11:00 A.M.
6. シドニー (Sydney)	3:30 P.M.

C Listen to the dialogues between Mr. Tanaka and a telephone operator. Find out the telephone numbers of the following people. W01-C

(Example) すずき	51-6751
1. かわさき	905-0877
2. リー (Lee)	5934-1026
3. ウッズ (Woods)	49-1509
4. クマール (Kumar)	67 82-3333

D Two students, Akira and Kate, are talking. Mark each of the following statements with ◯ if true, or ✕ if false. W01-D

1. (◯) Akira is a first-year student.
2. (✕) Akira is a student at the University of America.
3. (✕) Akira's major is history.
4. (✕) Kate is a second-year student.
5. (◯) Kate's major is Japanese.

Japanese Writing System —2 *Katakana* 🔊 W-JWS2

1. Listen to the audio and study the *katakana* characters.
2. When you have familiarized yourself with the characters, cut out the cards along the solid lines and practice reading each *katakana*, and check against the romanization on the back.

	a	*i*	*u*	*e*	*o*
	ア	イ	ウ	エ	オ
k	カ	キ	ク	ケ	コ
s	サ	シ	ス	セ	ソ
t	タ	チ	ツ	テ	ト
n	ナ	ニ	ヌ	ネ	ノ
h	ハ	ヒ	フ	ヘ	ホ
m	マ	ミ	ム	メ	モ
y	ヤ		ユ		ヨ
r	ラ	リ	ル	レ	ロ
w	ワ				ヲ
	ン				

o	e	u	i	a
ko	ke	ku	ki	ka
so	se	su	shi	sa
to	te	tsu	chi	ta
no	ne	nu	ni	na
ho	he	fu	hi	ha
mo	me	mu	mi	ma
yo		yu		ya
ro	re	ru	ri	ra
o (wo)				wa
				n

第2課 1 すうじ (Numbers)

I Read or listen to the following numbers and write them in Arabic numerals. 🔊 W02-1

(a) よんひゃくななじゅう __470__ (e) さんぜんろっぴゃくじゅうに __3612__

(b) はっぴゃくごじゅうさん __853__ (f) ごせんひゃくきゅうじゅうはち __5198__

(c) せんさんびゃく __1,300__ (g) よんまんろくせんきゅうひゃく __36900__

(d) いちまんななせん __17,000__ (h) きゅうまんにひゃくじゅう __92010__

II Write the following numbers in *hiragana*.

1. 541 __ごひゃくよんじゅういち__

2. 2,736 __にせんななひゃくさんじゅうろく__

3. 8,900 __はっせんきゅうひゃく__

4. 12,345 __まんにせんさんびゃくよんじゅうご__

III Look at the pictures and complete the dialogues.

¥160 ¥24,000 ¥3,600

1. Q：__じてんしゃは いくら ですか。__

   A：にまんよんせんえんです。

2. Q：かばんは いくらですか。

   A：__さんぜん ろっぴゃく えん です。__

3. Q：しんぶんは いくらですか。

   A：__ひゃく ろく じゅう えん です。__

第2課　2　これ / それ / あれ

☛Grammar 1

I Look at the pictures and translate the sentences into Japanese.

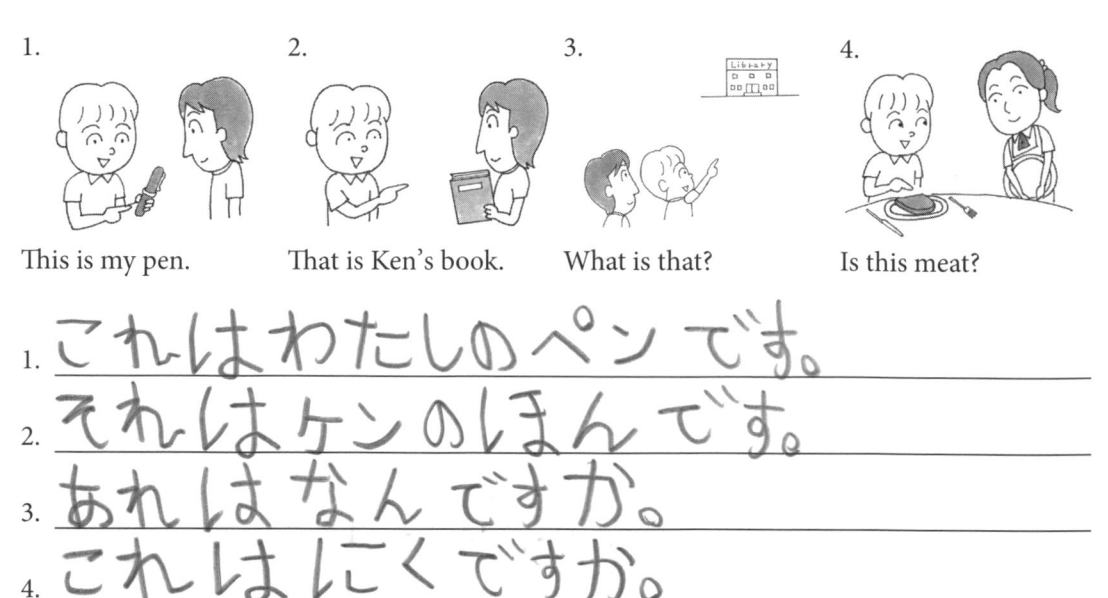

1. This is my pen.
2. That is Ken's book.
3. What is that?
4. Is this meat?

1. これはわたしのペンです。
2. それはケンのほんです。
3. あれはなんですか。
4. これはにくですか。

II Mary and Takeshi are talking. Look at the picture and fill the blanks with これ, それ, or あれ.

メアリー： 1. これ　　　は たけしさんの かさですか。

たけし： いいえ、 2. それ　　　は ゆいさんの かさです。

3. これ　　　は メアリーさんの さいふですか。

メアリー： はい、わたしの さいふです。

たけしさん、 4. あれ　　　は たけしさんの じてんしゃですか。

たけし： はい、そうです。

メアリー： 5. あれ　　　は なんですか。

たけし： ゆうびんきょくです。

第2課　だいにか　3　この / その / あの　☞Grammar 2

▶ Complete the following conversation between the attendant and the customer at a watch shop.

(3)
¥1,500

(1)
¥3,000

(2)
¥2,800

Attendant:　いらっしゃいませ。

Customer (*pointing at watch (1)*):　1. このとけいはいくらですか。
　　　　　　　　　　　　　　　　　　　(How much is this watch?)

Attendant:　そのとけいは　さんぜんえんです。

Customer (*pointing at watch (2)*):　2. そのとけいはいくらですか。
　　　　　　　　　　　　　　　　　　　(How much is that watch?)

Attendant:　3. このとけいはにせんはっびゃくです。

Customer (*pointing at watch (3)*):　4. あのとけいはいくらですか。
　　　　　　　　　　　　　　　　　　　(How much is that watch?)

Attendant:　5. あのとけいはせんこひゃくです。

Customer (*decided on (3)*):　6. じゃああのとけいをください。
　　　　　　　　　　　　　　　　(Then, I'll take that watch.)

第2課　4　ここ / そこ / あそこ・だれの　　☛Grammar 3・4

Ⅰ You are B. Answer A's questions with ここ, そこ, or あそこ.

1. A： たけしさんは どこですか。
   B： <u>たけしさんはあそこです。</u>

2. A： ソラさんは どこですか。
   B： <u>ソラさんはそこ です。</u>

3. A： ロバートさんは どこですか。
   B： <u>ロバートさんはここです。</u>

4. A： トイレは どこですか。
   B： <u>トイレはあそこ ですよ。</u>

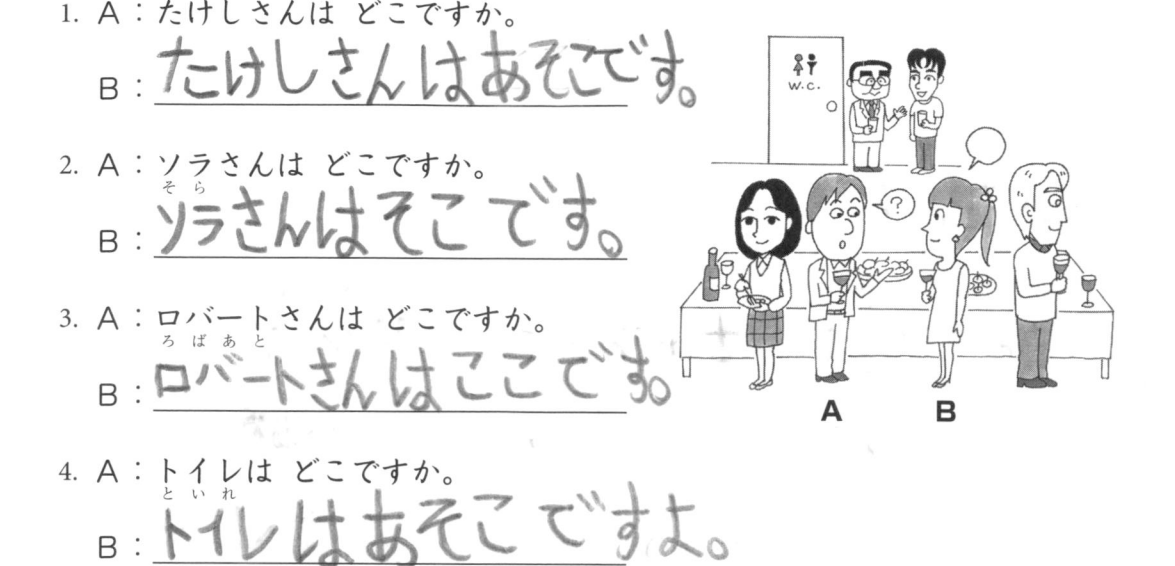

Ⅱ Kaoru asks Yui about the things that their friends have left in his room.

かおる　　　　　　　　ゆい

1. かおる： <u>これはだれのぼうしですか。</u>

   ゆい： それは たけしさんの ぼうしです。

2. かおる： <u>これはだれのさいふでか。</u>

   ゆい： それは わたしの さいふです。

3. かおる： <u>あれはだれのかさですか。</u>

   ゆい： あれは メアリーさんの かさです。

第2課 だいにか 5 Noun も・Noun じゃないです ☞Grammar 5・6

Ⅰ Translate the following sentences into Japanese. Use も after the underlined phrases.

1. Ms. Tanaka is Japanese. Mr. Yoshida is Japanese, too.

たなかさんはにほんじんです。よしださんもにほんじんです。

2. Ms. Tanaka is twenty years old. Mr. Yoshida is twenty years old, too.

たなかさんは はたちです。よしださんもはたちです。

3. This umbrella is 2,000 yen. That umbrella is 2,000 yen, too.

ぼくのかさはにせん¥です。そのかさもにせん¥です。

4. This is my bicycle. That is my bicycle, too.

これはわたしのじでんしゃです。それもわたしのじでんしゃです。

5. Takeshi's major is history. My major is history, too.

たけしのせんこうはれきしです。ぼくのせんこうもれきしです。

Ⅱ Answer the following questions in the negative.

1. たけしさんは かいしゃいん (office worker) ですか。

いいえ、たけしさんは かいしゃいんじゃありません。

2. たけしさんは アメリカじんですか。

いいえ、たけしさんはアメリカじんじゃないです。

3. たけしさんの せんこうは けいざいですか。

いいえ、たけしさんのせんこうは けいざいじゃありません。

4. これは たけしさんの かさですか。

いいえ、それはたけしさんのかさじゃありません。

5. これは たけしさんの ほんですか。

いいえ、それはたけしさんのほんじゃないです。

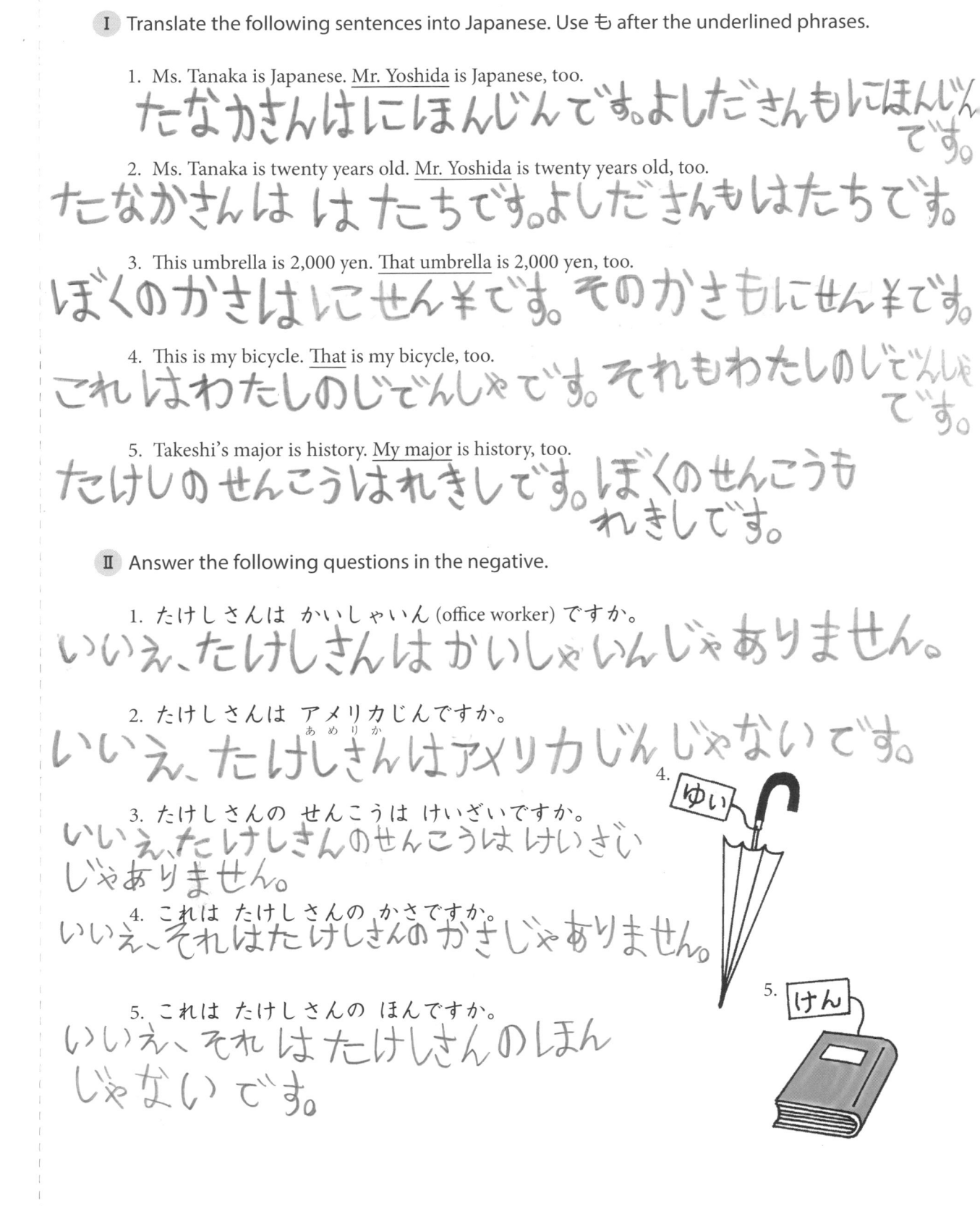

第2課　6　こたえましょう (Questions)
だいにか

▶ Answer the following questions in Japanese.

1. にほんじんですか。

2. にねんせいですか。

3. じゅうきゅうさいですか。

4. せんこうは けいざいですか。

5. おかあさんは にほんじんですか。

6. にほんごの ほんは いくらですか。

第2課 7 きくれんしゅう (Listening Comprehension)

A Listen to the dialogue at a kiosk and find out the prices of the following items. If you can't find out the price, indicate such with a question mark (?). ◀)) W02-A

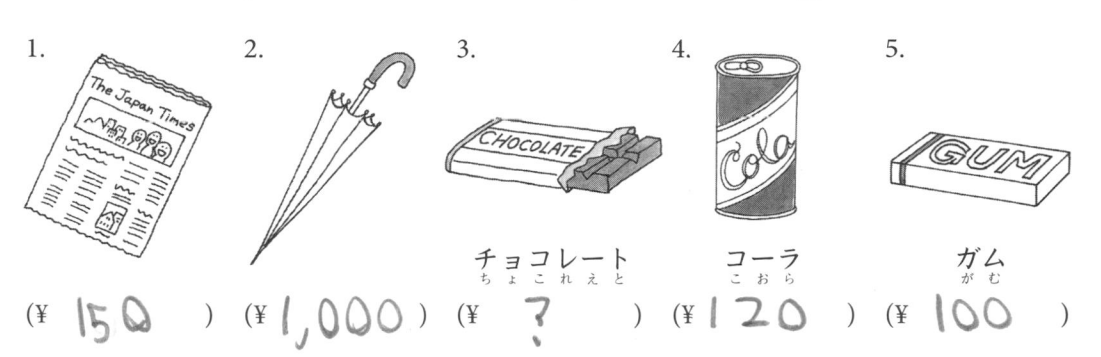

1. (¥ 150) 2. (¥ 1,000) 3. チョコレート (¥ ?) 4. コーラ (¥ 120) 5. ガム (¥ 100)

B Mary introduces her friend, Christy, to Takeshi. Answer the following questions in Japanese. ◀)) W02-B

＊フランス (France)

1. クリスティさんは アメリカじんですか。

いいえ、クリスティさんは アメリカじんじゃ ないです。クリスティさん フランスじん です。

2. クリスティさんの せんこうは なんですか。

クリスティさんの せんこうは えいご です。

3. クリスティさんの おとうさんは にほんじんですか。

はい、クリスティさんの おとうさんは にほんじん です。

4. クリスティさんの おかあさんは にほんじんですか。

いいえ、クリスティさんの おかあさんは にほんじんじゃありません。クリスティさんの おかあさんは フランスじん です。

C Mary and Takeshi are looking at the menu at a Japanese restaurant. ◀)) W02-C

1. How much are these items?

a. すきやき (¥ 3000) b. うどん (¥ 600) c. てんぷら (¥ 1200)
(beef & veggie hotpot) (wheat noodles) (deep-fried food)

2. Mark each of the following statements with ◯ if true, or with ✕ if false.

a. (✕) *Sukiyaki* has fish in it.

b. (◯) Mary thinks *sukiyaki* is expensive.

c. (◯) Both Takeshi and Mary ordered *udon*.

第3課　1　Verb Conjugation

☞Grammar 1

➤ Memorize the thirteen verbs introduced in Lesson 3. Read the explanation about verb conjugation and complete the following tables.

Ru-verbs

	dictionary form	present affirmative	present negative
1. get up	おきる	おきます	おきません
2. see	みる	みます	みません
3. eat	たべる	たべます	たべません
4. sleep	ねる	ねます	ねません

U-verbs

	dictionary form	present affirmative	present negative
5. speak	はなす	はなします	はなしませ
6. listen	きく	ききます	ききません
7. go	いく	いきます	いきません
8. read	よむ	よみます	よみません
9. drink	のむ	のみます	のみません
10. return	かえる	かえります	かえりません

Irregular Verbs

	dictionary form	present affirmative	present negative
11. come	くる	きます	きません
12. do	する	します	しません
13. study	べんきょうする	べんきょうしま	べんきょうしません

第3課　2　Noun を Verb　　　　　☛ Grammar 3

➤ Write a ます and ません sentence using two of the nouns in each group and a verb of your choice.

Example
Noun:　さかな　　にく　　やさい

affirmative　→　わたしは やさいを たべます。
negative　→　わたしは にくを たべません。

1.　Noun:　おさけ　　おちゃ　　コーヒー

affirmative　→わたしはおちゃ をのみます。
negative　→わたしはコーヒーをのみません。

2.　Noun:　にほんの えいが　　アメリカの えいが　　インド (India) の えいが

affirmative　→わたしは アメリカ のえいがを みます。
negative　→わたしはにほんのえいがをみません。

3.　Noun:　テニス　　サッカー (soccer)　　バスケットボール (basketball)

affirmative　→わたしは バスケットボールをみます。
negative　→わたしは テニスをみません

4.　Noun:　ほん　　おんがくの ざっし　　スポーツの ざっし

affirmative　→わたしはほんをよみます。
negative　→わたしはスポーツのざっしよみません。

5.　Noun:　にほんの おんがく　　ロック (rock)　　クラシック (classic)

affirmative　→わたしは ロックをききます。
negative　→わたしは クラシックをききません。

第3課　3　Verbs with Places　　　　　　　　☞Grammar 3

I Where do the following activities take place? Add the places and appropriate particles to the following sentences.

(Example) としょかんで ほんを よみます。

1. としょかんで_____べんきょうします。
2. うちで_____テレビを みます。
3. カフェで_____コーヒーを のみます。
4. えいがに_____いきます。
5. うちに_____かえります。

II Translate the following sentences into Japanese.

1. Mr. Tanaka will go to the library.

たなかさんはとしょかんにいきます。

2. My friend will come to Japan.

わたしのともだちはにほんにきます。

3. Mr. Suzuki listens to music at home.

すずきさんはいえでおんがくをききます。

4. I speak Japanese at home.

わたしはいえでにほんごをはなします。

5. I don't eat lunch at school.

わたしはがっこうでひるはんをたべません

第3課 4 Time References　　　　　　　　　☞ Grammar 4

I Time Expressions—Read Grammar 4 (p. 90) on time references, and classify the words below into two groups. If the words are always used with に, write に after the words.

1. こんばん <u>X</u>
2. しゅうまつ <u>(に)</u>
3. あさ <u>(に)</u>
4. いつ <u>X</u>
5. きょう <u>X</u>
6. いま <u>X</u>
7. どようび <u>に</u>
8. あした <u>X</u>
9. じゅういちじ <u>に</u>
10. まいにち <u>X</u>
11. まいばん <u>X</u>

II Your Day—Describe what you do on a typical day. Include descriptions of the activities listed below. Whenever possible, include place and time expressions. Refer to Grammar 7 (p. 91) on the basic order of phrases.

おきる　　いく　　たべる　　べんきょうする　　かえる　　ねる

1. わたしは まいにち <u>ろく</u> じに <u>おき</u> ます。
2. わたしはまいにちごごいちじにしごとにいきます。
3. わたしはまいにちごごさんじにたべます。
4. わたしはまいにちべんきょうしません。
5. わたしはまいばんごごしゅうじにねます。

III Translate the following sentences into Japanese.

1. I speak Japanese every day.

わたしはまいにちにほんごをはなします。

2. I will not watch TV tonight.

わたしはごんばんテレビをみません。

3. Takeshi does not come to school on Saturdays.

たけしさんはどようびにがっこうをきません。

第3課 5 Suggestion Using ～ませんか   ☛Grammar 5

I Review Practice V-C (p. 99) and translate the following conversation.

メアリー：1. _____
                    (Would you like to see a movie tonight?)

たけし： 2. _____
                    (Tonight is not a very good time . . .)

            3. _____
                    (How about tomorrow?)

メアリー：4. _____
                    (Sounds great.)

II Imagine you ask someone out. Write the dialogue between you and your friend.

You: 1. _____

Friend: 2. _____

You: 3. _____

Friend: 4. _____

第3課　6　Frequency Adverbs

☛ Grammar 6

➤ Translate the following sentences into Japanese.

1. I often go to the library.

   わたしは ＿＿＿＿＿＿＿ としょかん ＿＿＿＿ ＿＿＿＿＿＿＿＿＿ 。

2. Yumi often comes to my house.

3. I usually get up at six.

4. Professor Yamashita usually goes to sleep at eleven.

5. I sometimes read Japanese newspapers.

6. Takeshi sometimes drinks coffee at that cafe.

7. Yui does not eat much.

第3課 7 答えましょう (Questions)
こた

▶ Answer the following questions in Japanese.

1. よく スポーツを しますか。

2. よく えいがを みますか。

3. よく なにを のみますか。

4. おんがくは よく なにを ききますか。

5. どこで べんきょうしますか。

6. しゅうまつは よく どこに いきますか。

7. しゅうまつは よく なにを しますか。

8. なんじごろ おきますか。

9. なんじごろ ねますか。

第3課 | 8 | 聞く練習 (Listening Comprehension)

A Listen to the dialogue between Sora and Mary. Where will they be? What will they do? Choose from the list below. 🔊 W03-A　　　　＊レストラン (restaurant)

		Saturday		Sunday	
		Where	What	Where	What
🙂	Mary				
🙂	Sora				

Where:

a. school	b. library	c. home
d. Osaka	e. Tokyo	f. Kyoto

What:

g. read a book	h. play sports	i. study
j. see a movie	k. eat dinner	

B Listen to the dialogue at an evening meeting at a summer camp. The group leader and the students are discussing the schedule for the next day. Complete the schedule below.

🔊 W03-B

＊スケジュール (schedule)　ヨガ (yoga)

1. 6:00 A.M. ( )	6. 3:00 P.M. ( )
2. 7:30 ( )	7. 6:00 ( )
3. 9:00 ( )	8. 7:30 ( )
4. 12:30 P.M. ( )	9. 11:30 ( )
5. 1:30 ( )	

a. breakfast	b. dinner	c. get up
d. go to bed	e. lunch	f. do yoga
g. play tennis	h. study	i. watch a movie

C Listen to the dialogue between Sora and her friend. How often does she do the following things? ◀)) W03-C

(A = every day / B = often / C = sometimes / D = not often / E = not at all)

1. (   ) study Japanese
2. (   ) go to the library
3. (   ) watch American movies
4. (   ) watch Japanese movies
5. (   ) play tennis
6. (   ) drink coffee

D Listen to the dialogue between Mary and a Japanese friend and answer the questions below. ◀)) W03-D

1. What did the man suggest first?　(   )

    a. Coffee at a cafe   b. Beer at a bar   c. Coffee at his place   d. Lunch

2. What time is it?　(   )

    a. 8 o'clock   b. 9 o'clock   c. 10 o'clock   d. 11 o'clock

3. What is Mary's excuse for declining the suggestion? (Mark ◯ for all that apply.)

    a. (   ) She needs to go back home.

    b. (   ) It is too late.

    c. (   ) She needs to study.

    d. (   ) She needs to go to sleep early.

4. What other suggestions did the man make? (Mark ◯ for all that apply.)

    a. (   ) Reading Japanese books together

    b. (   ) Practicing Japanese at a cafe

    c. (   ) Having lunch together the next day

    d. (   ) Walking her home

第4課 | 1　Xがあります / います　　　　　　　　　☛Grammar 1

Ⅰ Translate the following sentences into Japanese.

1. There is a bus stop over there.

2. There will be no class on Thursday.

3. I do not have a bicycle. (lit., There is not a bicycle.)

4. There is Professor Yamashita over there.

5. I have a child. (lit., There is a child.)

Ⅱ Answer the following questions in Japanese.

1. あした、アルバイトがありますか。

2. いつ日本語のクラスがありますか。
　　　　に ほん ご

3. 日本に友だちがいますか。
　　に ほん　　　とも

4. 兄弟 (brothers and sisters) がいますか。
　　きょうだい

おねえさん : older sister
いもうと : younger sister
おにいさん : older brother
おとうと : younger brother

第4課　2　Describing Where Things Are

☛Grammar 2

Ⅰ Draw a picture showing the items mentioned in the passage below, each in correct geometrical relation to the others.

スマホはつくえの上です。時計もつくえの上です。
帽子はスマホと時計の間です。かばんはつくえの下です。
つくえはテレビの近くです。

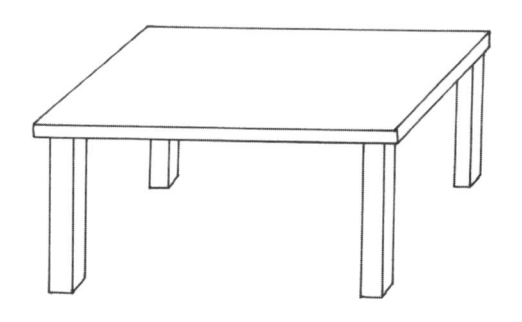

Ⅱ Look at the pictures and answer the following questions.

1. 雑誌はどこですか。

2. メアリーさんの傘はどこですか。

3. 日本語の本はどこですか。

4. 図書館はどこですか。

5. 銀行はどこですか。

1.　magazine

2.　Mary's umbrella

3.　Japanese book

4. 5.

第4課 3 **Past Tense** (Nouns)   ☛Grammar 3

Ⅰ Answer the following questions.

1. きのうは月曜日でしたか。
   _{げつようび}

2. きのうは十五日でしたか。
   _{じゅう ご にち}

3. 今日の朝ご飯はハンバーガーでしたか。
   _{きょう} _{あさ} _{はん}

4. 子供の時、いい子供でしたか。
   _{こ ども} _{とき} _{こ ども}

Ⅱ Translate the following sentences into Japanese.

1. My bicycle was 30,000 yen.

2. Yesterday was Sunday.

3. Teacher's major was not English.

4. Professor Yamashita was not a Nihon University student.

第4課　4　Verb Conjugation (Past Tense)　☛Grammar 4

▶ Fill in the conjugation table below. If you are unclear about the *u*-verb/*ru*-verb distinction, read Grammar 1 in Lesson 3 (pp. 86-88) once again. If you are unclear about the past tense conjugation, refer to the table on p. 110.

U-verbs

	dictionary form	past affirmative	past negative
1. drink			
2. speak			
3. listen			
4. buy			
5. take			
6. write			
7. wait			
8. there is (a thing)			

Ru-verbs and Irregular Verbs

	dictionary form	past affirmative	past negative
9. eat			
10. get up			
11. do			
12. come			

第4課　5　**Past Tense** (Verbs)　　　　　　　　👉Grammar 4

I The pictures below show what Takeshi did last weekend. Answer the following questions in Japanese.

Friday	**Saturday**	**Sunday**

home	supermarket	town

1. たけしさんは金曜日（きんようび）に音楽（おんがく）を聞（き）きましたか。

2. たけしさんは土曜日（どようび）にどこでアルバイトをしましたか。

3. たけしさんはいつレポートを書（か）きましたか。

4. たけしさんは日曜日（にちようび）に何（なに）をしましたか。(Fill in the blanks.)

　　　_____で_____と_____を

　　　_____。

5. あなたは、週末（しゅうまつ）、何（なに）をしましたか。

II Translate the following sentences into Japanese.

1. Yumi did not take pictures at all.

2. I often ate hamburgers when I was a child.

3. Takeshi did not study much when he was in high school.

第4課　6　も

☛ Grammar 5

▶ Translate the sentences into Japanese. Note that the particle も replaces は, が, and を, but goes side by side with other particles.

1. Mary went to the park. Takeshi went to the park, too.

2. There is a bookstore over there. There is a restaurant, too.

3. I drink tea. I drink coffee, too.

4. Ken will go to Korea. He will go to China, too.

5. Yui ate ice cream on Friday. She ate ice cream on Saturday, too.

6. Yumi studied at the library yesterday. She studied at home, too.

7. I took pictures at school yesterday. I took pictures at home, too.

第4課　7　〜時間・Particles

👉 Grammar 6

Ⅰ Translate the following sentences into Japanese.

1. Mary <u>watched TV</u> <u>for two hours</u> <u>yesterday</u>.
　　　　(3)　　　　　　(2)　　　　　(1)

メアリーさんは ＿＿＿＿＿＿ ＿＿＿＿＿＿ ＿＿＿＿＿＿＿＿＿。
　　　　　　　　　　(1)　　　　　　(2)　　　　　　　(3)

2. Takeshi <u>waited for Mary</u> <u>for one hour</u> <u>in front of the convenience store</u>.
　　　　　(3)　　　　　　　(2)　　　　　　(1)

たけしさんは ＿＿＿＿＿＿＿＿＿＿＿ ＿＿＿＿＿＿＿
　　　　　　　　　　　(1)　　　　　　　　　(2)

＿＿＿＿＿＿＿＿＿＿＿＿＿＿＿＿。
　　　　　　(3)

3. Sora <u>studies Japanese</u> <u>at the library</u> <u>for about one hour</u> <u>every day</u>.
　　　　(4)　　　　　　　(3)　　　　　　(2)　　　　　(1)

ソラさんは ＿＿＿＿＿＿＿＿＿ ＿＿＿＿＿＿＿＿＿＿
　　　　　　　　　(1)　　　　　　　　　(2)

＿＿＿＿＿＿＿＿＿＿＿ ＿＿＿＿＿＿＿＿＿＿＿＿＿。
　　　　　(3)　　　　　　　　　　(4)

Ⅱ Fill in the particles that are missing. You may want to refer to the Vocabulary section (p. 105), where the particle that goes with each of the new verbs is shown in the parentheses.

1. 私はあした友だち＿＿＿＿会います。

2. メアリーさんは京都のお寺で写真＿＿＿＿撮りました。

3. 私は図書館の前でロバートさん＿＿＿＿待ちました。

4. スーパーで肉＿＿＿＿買いました。

5. 私は中国語＿＿＿＿わかりません。

6. 私の町＿＿＿＿日本のレストラン＿＿＿＿あります。

第4課　8　答えましょう (Questions)

▶ Answer the following questions in Japanese.

1. あなたの家はどこですか。

2. あなたの町に本屋がありますか。

3. 猫／犬がいますか。名前は何ですか。

4. 今日は何曜日ですか。

5. きのう、だれと晩ご飯を食べましたか。

6. きのう、何時間勉強しましたか。

7. 何曜日に日本語のクラスがありますか。

8. 先週の週末、何をしましたか。

第4課 9 聞く練習 (Listening Comprehension)

A Mary is showing a picture that she took at a party. Identify the following people. 🔊 W04-A

1. (　　　) Ken
2. (　　　) Rika
3. (　　　) Mike
4. (　　　) Takeshi
5. (　　　) Mother
6. (　　　) Father

a
b
c
d
e
f

B Mary is talking with her homestay father at night. Listen to the dialogue and answer the questions in Japanese. 🔊 W04-B

1. お父さんは今日何をしましたか。　_____

2. お母さんは何をしましたか。　_____

3. メアリーさんとお父さんはあした何をしますか。　_____

C Listen to the dialogue in the classroom and answer the following questions. 🔊 W04-C

＊カラオケ (karaoke)　テスト (test)

1. What is the date today?

　a. September 10　　b. September 13　　c. September 14　　d. September 18

2. What day is today?

　a. Sunday　　　b. Monday　　　c. Tuesday　　　d. Wednesday

　e. Thursday　　f. Friday　　　g. Saturday

3. Who did these things? Mark ◯ for the things they did.

	studied	took photos	went to Tokyo	read a book	went to karaoke	did shopping
Sora						
Mary						
Robert						

第5課　1　Adjective Conjugation (Present Tense)　　☞Grammar 1

▶ Fill in the conjugation table below.

い-adjectives

	dictionary form	present affirmative	present negative
1. large			
2. expensive			
3. frightening			
4. interesting			
5. old			
6. good			

な-adjectives

	dictionary form	present affirmative	present negative
7. quiet			
8. beautiful			
9. healthy			
10. fond of			
11. disgusted			
12. lively			

第5課 2 Adjectives (Present Tense)   ☛ Grammar 1

I Answer the questions.

1. 日本語の宿題はやさしいですか。

2. 今日は忙しいですか。

3. あなたの部屋はきれいですか。

4. 日本語のクラスはおもしろいですか。

5. あなたの町は静かですか。

II Translate the following sentences into Japanese.

1. This watch is expensive.

2. This coffee is not delicious.

3. Professor Yamashita is energetic.

4. The weather is not good.

5. I will not be free tomorrow.

▼ Fill in the conjugation table below.

い-adjectives

	present affirmative	present negative	past affirmative	past negative
1. あたらしい				
2. いそがしい				
3. さむい				
4. むずかしい				
5. ちいさい				
6. いい				

な-adjectives

	present affirmative	present negative	past affirmative	past negative
7. ひま（な）				
8. にぎやか（な）				
9. すき（な）				
10. きれい（な）				

クラス [　　　]　なまえ [　　　]

第5課 4 **Adjectives** (Past Tense)   ☛Grammar 2

Ⅰ Answer the questions.

1. 先週はひまでしたか。
   せんしゅう

2. テストは難しかったですか。
   むずか

3. きのうは暑かったですか。
   あつ

4. 週末は楽しかったですか。
   しゅうまつ　たの

5. きのうの晩ご飯はおいしかったですか。
   ばん　はん

Ⅱ Translate the following sentences into Japanese.

1. I was busy yesterday.

2. The homework was difficult.

3. Takeshi's room was not clean.

4. The weather was good.

5. The trip was not fun.

6. The hotel was not expensive.

第5課　5　Adjective ＋ Noun　　　　　☛Grammar 3

I Look at the pictures and answer the questions.

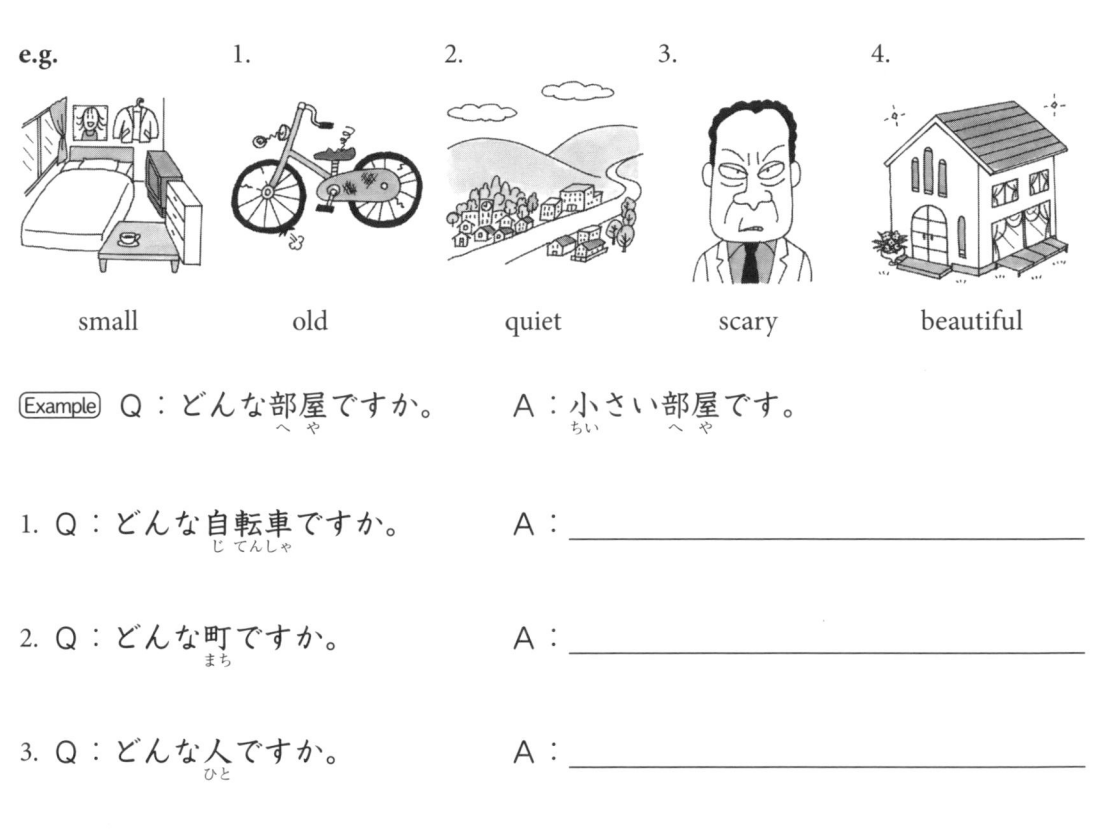

e.g.　　　　　1.　　　　　2.　　　　　3.　　　　　4.

small　　　old　　　quiet　　　scary　　　beautiful

(Example) Q：どんな部屋ですか。　　A：小さい部屋です。

1. Q：どんな自転車ですか。　　A：＿＿＿＿＿＿＿＿＿＿＿＿＿

2. Q：どんな町ですか。　　A：＿＿＿＿＿＿＿＿＿＿＿＿＿

3. Q：どんな人ですか。　　A：＿＿＿＿＿＿＿＿＿＿＿＿＿

4. Q：どんな家ですか。　　A：＿＿＿＿＿＿＿＿＿＿＿＿＿

II Translate the following sentences.

1. I met a kind person.

2. I bought delicious fruit.

3. I read an interesting book last week.

第5課 6 好き (な) / きらい (な)

☛ Grammar 4

➤ Write sentences stating whether you like/dislike the things below. Use 好き (な) for "like" and きらい (な) for "don't like." Use 大〜 for emphasis.

[Example] homework → 私は宿題が大好きです。
わたし　しゅくだい　だいす

1. Japanese class

   →

2. this town

   →

3. Mondays

   →

4. ocean

   →

5. cats

   →

6. cold mornings

   →

7. fish

   →

8. frightening movies

   →

9. (your own sentence)

   →

第5課 7 〜ましょう / 〜ましょうか   ☛Grammar 5

Ⅰ You and your friend will spend one day together. Complete the underlined parts with 〜ましょう.

友だち：どこに行きますか。

私：　　1.＿＿＿＿＿＿＿＿＿＿＿＿＿＿＿＿＿＿＿＿＿＿＿＿＿＿＿＿＿

友だち：いいですね。そこで何をしますか。

私：　　2.＿＿＿＿＿＿＿＿＿＿＿＿＿＿＿＿＿＿＿＿＿。それから、

　　　　3.＿＿＿＿＿＿＿＿＿＿＿＿＿＿＿＿＿＿＿＿＿＿＿＿＿＿＿＿＿

友だち：何時に会いますか。

私：　　4.＿＿＿＿＿＿＿＿＿＿＿＿＿＿＿＿＿＿＿＿＿＿＿＿＿＿＿＿＿

Ⅱ Translate the following sentences into Japanese.

1. Let's wait for the bus.

2. Let's go out together.

3. Let's take pictures here.

4. Shall we watch this movie tonight?

5. This homework is difficult. Shall we ask our teacher?

第5課 8 答えましょう (Questions)

I Answer the following questions in Japanese regarding your best trip.

1. どこに行きましたか。

2. だれと行きましたか。

3. 天気はどうでしたか。

4. 食べ物はどうでしたか。

5. そこで何をしましたか。

6. おみやげを買いましたか。

II Answer the following questions in Japanese.

1. どんな食べ物が好きですか。

2. どんな飲み物が好きですか。

3. どんな音楽が好きですか。

第5課 9 聞く練習 (Listening Comprehension)
き れんしゅう

A Listen to the dialogue between a real estate agent and her customer and choose the appropriate answers. 🔊 W05-A   ＊一か月 (one month)
いっ　げつ

1. The house is [a. new / b. old].

2. The house is [a. clean / b. not clean].

3. The house is [a. quiet / b. not quiet].

4. The rooms are [a. big / b. not big].

5. There are [a. many / b. not many] rooms.

6. The rent is [a. 90,400 / b. 94,000] yen a month.

B Listen to the TV game show "Who's My Date?" Three men want to invite Ms. Suzuki on a date. 🔊 W05-B   ＊おめでとうございます (Congratulations.)

1. Fill in the blanks in Japanese.

	Favorite type	What he does on holidays
吉田 よし だ		
川口 かわぐち		
中山 なかやま		

2. Who did Ms. Suzuki choose?   [a. 吉田   b. 川口   c. 中山]
よし だ   かわぐち   なかやま

C Listen to the interview with Mary and Takeshi and fill in the chart with the following letters: A = likes / B = doesn't like very much / C = hates. 🔊 W05-C

	J-Pop （Jポップ）	Rock （ロック）	Classical music （クラシック）	Animation （アニメ）	Horror movies （ホラー）
👧 Mary					
👦 Takeshi					

第6課　1　*Te*-form —1

☞Grammar 1

➤ Review the Vocabulary section (pp. 148-149) and Grammar 1 (pp. 150-151), and fill in the following table.

Ru-verbs

	dictionary form	*te*-form	long form（〜ます）
1. open			
2. close			
3. teach			
4. forget			
5. get off			
6. borrow			
7. take a shower			
8. turn on			

U-verbs

	dictionary form	*te*-form	long form（〜ます）
9. smoke			
10. use			
11. help			

	dictionary form	*te*-form	long form（〜ます）
12. hurry			

	dictionary form	*te*-form	long form （〜ます）
13. return (a thing)			
14. turn off			

15. stand up			
16. carry			

17. die			

18. play			

19. be absent			

20. sit down			
21. enter			

Irregular Verbs

	dictionary form	*te*-form	long form （〜ます）
22. bring (a person)			
23. bring (a thing)			
24. call			

第6課　2　*Te*-form —2　　　　　　👉Grammar 1

❯ Review Grammar 1 (pp. 150-151) and conjugate the verbs below into their respective *te*-forms. The numbers indicate the lesson in which the verbs first appeared.

Ru-verbs

1. おきる (3)　→
2. たべる (3)　→
3. ねる (3)　→
4. みる (3)　→
5. いる (4)　→
6. でかける (5) →

U-verbs ending with う

7. あう (4)　→
8. かう (4)　→

U-verbs ending with く

9. きく (3)　→
10. かく (4)　→

U-verb ending with く (irregular)

11. いく (3)　→

U-verb ending with ぐ

12. およぐ (5) →

U-verb ending with す

13. はなす (3)　→

U-verb ending with つ

14. まつ (4)　→

U-verbs ending with む

15. のむ (3)　→
16. よむ (3)　→

U-verbs ending with る

17. かえる (3)　→
18. ある (4)　→
19. とる (4)　→
20. わかる (4)　→
21. のる (5)　→
22. やる (5)　→

Irregular Verbs

23. くる (3)　→
24. する (3)　→
25. べんきょうする (3) →

第6課　3　〜てください

☛Grammar 2

Ⅰ Write what each person says using 〜てください.

1.

take a picture

2.

teach this kanji

3.

carry this bag

4.

use this towel（タオル）

5.

sit down

6.

bring a book

1. _____

2. _____

3. _____

4. _____

5. _____

6. _____

Ⅱ Write three request sentences using 〜てください. Indicate in the parentheses who you are going to ask to do those things.

1. (　　　　　　　　) _____

2. (　　　　　　　　) _____

3. (　　　　　　　　) _____

第6課　4　Describing Two Activities

☞Grammar 3

Ⅰ The pictures below describe what Takeshi did yesterday. Make sentences using *te*-forms.

1.

2

3.

4.

1. _____

2. _____

3. _____

4. _____

Ⅱ Translate the following sentences.

1. I will go home and rest.

2. Mary and Takeshi met and talked for about an hour.

3. Let's go to the sea and swim.

第6課　5　〜てもいいです　　　　　　　　☛Grammar 4

➤ Ask the following people if it is okay to do the following things, using 〜てもいいですか.

To your friend at your friend's apartment:

1. enter the room

2. look at the pictures

3. turn on the TV

4. (your own)

To your teacher in class:

5. go to the restroom

6. speak English

7. borrow a textbook

8. (your own)

第6課　6　〜てはいけません　　　　　　　☛Grammar 5

Ⅰ Look at the signs and make sentences using 〜てはいけません.

| 1. No Smoking | 2. Do Not Enter | 3. No Photographs | 4. No Food |

1. _____

2. _____

3. _____

4. _____

Ⅱ Describe three things that you are prohibited from doing at some places.

(Example) 寮 (dorm) でお酒を飲んではいけません。

1. _____

2. _____

3. _____

第6課　7　〜から・〜ましょうか　　　　　☞Grammar 6・7

I Translate the following sentences, using 〜から.

1. I am not free today. (It's) because I have a test tomorrow.

2. The test was not difficult. (That was) because I had studied a lot.

3. Let's go out tonight. (It's) because tomorrow is a holiday.

4. I helped my mother. (It's) because she was busy.

5. I will not drink coffee. (It's) because I drank coffee in the morning.

II Complete the dialogues for the following situations using 〜ましょうか.

1.

A :＿＿＿＿＿＿＿＿＿＿＿＿＿＿＿＿＿＿＿＿＿＿＿。

B：ありがとう。お願いします。
　　　　　　　　ねが

2.

A :＿＿＿＿＿＿＿＿＿＿＿＿＿＿＿＿＿＿＿＿＿＿＿。

B：すみません。お願いします。
　　　　　　　　　　ねが

3.

A :＿＿＿＿＿＿＿＿＿＿＿＿＿＿＿＿＿＿＿＿＿＿＿。

B：いいえ、大丈夫です。
　　　　　　だいじょうぶ

第6課　8　答えましょう (Questions)
こた

➤ Answer the following questions in Japanese.

1. 朝起きて、何をしますか。
あさ お　　なに

2. きのう、家に帰って何をしましたか。
いえ　かえ　なに

3. テストの時、教科書を見てもいいですか。
とき　きょうかしょ　み

4. 電車の中で何をしてはいけませんか。
でんしゃ　なか　なに

5. 子供の時、よく勉強しましたか。
こども　とき　べんきょう

6. 子供の時、よくゲームをしましたか。
こども　とき

7. 高校の時、よく何をしましたか。
こうこう　とき　　なに

第6課 9 聞く練習 (Listening Comprehension)
き れんしゅう

A Listen to the dialogue at a youth hostel. Mark each of the following statements with ○ if true, or with ✕ if false. ◀))) W06-A   ＊外 (outside)　コインランドリー (laundromat)
そと

1. (   ) Breakfast starts at 6:30.

2. (   ) Smoking is not permitted in the rooms.

3. (   ) You can take a shower in the morning.

4. (   ) There is no laundromat in this building.

B Robert is staying at a "smart hotel room" in Tokyo. Listen to his commands after "OK, My Room." Mark ○ for what he says. ◀))) W06-B

＊カーテン (curtain)　ライブのチケット (concert ticket)　了解しました (Certainly)
りょうかい

Robert asked:

1. (   ) close the window curtain   4. (   ) buy a concert ticket

2. (   ) turn on the room light   5. (   ) tell the time in Japan

3. (   ) turn on the TV   6. (   ) call his mother

C Takeshi is trying to organize a picnic. Listen to the dialogue and answer the questions in Japanese. ◀))) W06-C   ＊ピクニック (picnic)

1. When is NOT convenient for each of them? Why?

	a. Inconvenient day	b. Reasons
😊 ゆい		
😐 ソラ		
🙂 ロバート		

2. いつピクニックに行きますか。 _____
い

第7課 1 *Te*-form

▶ Identify the verbs as *u*-, *ru*-, or irregular verbs and fill in the table below.

	u/*ru*/irregular	long form	*te*-form
e.g. ある	*u*	あります	あって
1. わかる			
2. やる			
3. けす			
4. たつ			
5. おきる			
6. かえる			
7. くる			
8. する			
9. あそぶ			
10. きる			
11. かぶる			
12. わすれる			
13. はく			
14. うたう			
15. すむ			
16. けっこんする			

第7課 2 ～ている (Actions in Progress)　　　☛Grammar 1

Ⅰ Describe the following pictures, using ～ています.

1. _____

2. _____

3. _____

4. _____

5. _____

Ⅱ Answer the following questions in Japanese.

1. 今、何をしていますか。

2. きのうの午後八時ごろ何をしていましたか。

Ⅲ Translate the following sentences.

1. Mary is waiting for a bus at the bus stop.

2. At two o'clock yesterday, Takeshi was playing tennis with a friend.

3. I called home. My older sister was sleeping.

第7課　3　〜ている (Result of a Change)　☞Grammar 2

Ⅰ This is Yui's family. Answer the following questions in Japanese.

Father
51, lives in Nagano,
works at a bank

Mother
47, lives in Nagano,
works at a hospital

Older sister
23, lives in Tokyo,
college student,
married

Younger brother
16, lives in Nagano,
student

1. お父さんは何をしていますか。
　　とう　　　なに

2. お母さんは何をしていますか。
　　かあ　　　なに

3. お姉さんは働いていますか。
　　ねえ　　　はたら

4. お姉さんは結婚していますか。
　　ねえ　　　けっこん

5. お姉さんは長野に住んでいますか。
　　ねえ　　　なが の　　す

6. 弟さんはどこに住んでいますか。
　　おとうと　　　　　す

7. お父さんは何歳ですか。
　　とう　　　なんさい

Ⅱ Write about your family or friends. Try to use expressions you have learned in this lesson.

第7課 4 Describing People

☞ Grammar 3

I Translate the following sentences.

1. Yasuo is not tall.

2. Yasuo is very bright.

3. Norio is wearing a new T-shirt today.

4. Norio is thin, but Yasuo is overweight.

やすお　　のりお

II You are at a big shopping mall with your younger sister, but she is missing now. Report this to customer service and describe your sister.

1. Cap:

2. Hair:

3. Glasses:

4. Eyes:

5. Clothes (above the waistline):

6. Clothes (below the waistline):

第7課 5 Adjective/Noun *Te*-forms ☞Grammar 4

I Look at the following pictures and complete the sentences.

1.

inexpensive/delicious

2.

quiet/boring

3.
very small/cute

4.
very clean/new

5.

old/interesting

6.
long hair/large eyes

1. あのレストランの食べ物は＿＿＿＿＿＿＿＿＿＿＿＿＿＿＿＿＿＿＿。
    た　もの

2. 私の町は＿＿＿＿＿＿＿＿＿＿＿＿＿＿＿＿＿＿＿＿＿＿＿＿＿＿。
    わたし　まち

3. 私の猫は＿＿＿＿＿＿＿＿＿＿＿＿＿＿＿＿＿＿＿＿＿＿＿＿＿。
    わたし　ねこ

4. 私の部屋は＿＿＿＿＿＿＿＿＿＿＿＿＿＿＿＿＿＿＿＿＿＿＿＿。
    わたし　へ　や

5. このお寺は＿＿＿＿＿＿＿＿＿＿＿＿＿＿＿＿＿＿＿＿＿＿＿＿。
    てら

6. ななみさんは＿＿＿＿＿＿＿＿＿＿＿＿＿＿＿＿＿＿＿＿＿＿＿。

II Describe the following items, using two or more adjectives.

1. 日本は＿＿＿＿＿＿＿＿＿＿＿＿＿＿＿＿＿＿＿＿＿＿＿＿＿＿＿。
    に　ほん

2. 私は＿＿＿＿＿＿＿＿＿＿＿＿＿＿＿＿＿＿＿＿＿＿＿＿＿＿＿＿。
    わたし

3. 私の町は＿＿＿＿＿＿＿＿＿＿＿＿＿＿＿＿＿＿＿＿＿＿＿＿＿。
    わたし　まち

4. 私の友だちは＿＿＿＿＿＿＿＿＿＿＿＿＿＿＿＿＿＿＿＿＿＿＿。
    わたし　とも

第7課　6　Verb Stem ＋ に行く / 来る / 帰る
　　　　　　　　　　　　　　　　　　　　　　　　☛Grammar 5

Ⅰ　Rewrite the sentences below, using the stem ＋ に行く / 来る / 帰る pattern.

(Example)　図書館に行って、本を借ります。　→　図書館に本を借りに行きます。

1. 大阪に行って、友だちに会います。
　→

2. 家に帰って、晩ご飯を食べます。
　→

3. きのう、町に行って、雑誌を買いました。
　→

4. 私は週末京都に行って、写真を撮りました。
　→

5. ロバートさんはよく私のアパートに来て、パソコンを使います。
　→

Ⅱ　Make your own sentences, using a place from the list below.

e.g.							
大学	日本	食堂	コンビニ	友だちのうち	図書館	お寺	海

(Example)　大学　→　大学に友だちに会いに行きます。

1. _____

2. _____

3. _____

4. _____

第7課 7 Counting People　　　　　　　　　　☛Grammar 6

I Answer the questions in Japanese.

1. 兄弟がいますか。何人いますか。
   きょうだい　　　　　　なんにん

2. ルームメイト (roommate) がいますか。何人いますか。
   　　　　　　　　　　　　　　　　　　　なんにん

3. 日本語のクラスに学生が何人いますか。
   に ほん ご　　　　　　がくせい　なんにん

4. あなたの町に人が何人ぐらい住んでいますか。
   　　　　　まち　ひと　なんにん　　　す

5. 日本人の友だちが何人いますか。
   に ほんじん　とも　　　なんにん

II Translate the following sentences.

1. Q ： How many students are there in your school?

   A ： There are about 10,000 students in my school.

2. My older sister has two children.

第7課 8 答えましょう (Questions)

➤ Circle one person below and answer the questions in Japanese regarding him/her.

father	mother	friend	girlfriend	boyfriend

others (   )

1. 名前は何ですか。

2. 何歳ですか。

3. どこに住んでいますか。

4. 何をしていますか。

5. 結婚していますか。

6. 背が高いですか。

7. 髪が長いですか。

8. どんな人ですか。(describe two personality traits)

第7課 9 聞く練習 (Listening Comprehension)

き れんしゅう

A One student got robbed by someone at the dorm. A police officer is asking Robert what he and the other students were doing at the time of the incident. Write in Japanese what the following people were doing. 🔊 W07-A ＊ほかの (other)

1. ロバートさんとソラさんは、_____

2. たけしさんとけんさんは、_____

3. ゆいさんは、_____

B Listen to a TV reporter at a celebrity's party. Choose appropriate descriptions for each celebrity. 🔊 W07-B ＊ドレス (dress)　ボーイフレンド (boyfriend)

1. Uno Daiki 　　　　　　　　　(　　) (　　)

2. Noguchi Erika 　　　　　　　(　　) (　　)

3. Matsumoto Kana 　　　　　　(　　) (　　)

4. Matsumoto Kana's new boyfriend 　(　　) (　　)

| a. wears jeans | b. has short hair | c. wears glasses | d. wears a hat |
| e. has long hair | f. is cute | g. is fat | h. is tall |

C Mary is interviewing people who are walking downtown on Sunday. What is each interviewee doing today? Choose the correct answers. 🔊 W07-C

1. Tanaka: 　[a. buying flowers 　　 b. buying cards 　　 c. buying a game]

2. Sato: 　[a. playing games 　　 b. singing songs 　　 c. playing sports]

3. Suzuki: 　[a. working at a department store 　　 b. seeing his younger sister

　　　　　c. talking with his younger brother]

第8課　1　Short Forms (Present Tense)

☛Grammar 1

▶ Fill in the conjugation table below. Note that *ru*-verbs, *u*-verbs, and irregular verbs appear randomly on this sheet.

	dictionary form	short, negative	long, affirmative	*te*-form
e.g. eat	たべる	たべない	たべます	たべて
1. open				
2. buy				
3. sit down				
4. come				
5. die				
6. turn off				
7. study				
8. write				
9. there is (a thing)				
10. drink				
11. understand				
12. wait				
13. play				
14. hurry				

第8課　2　**Short Forms** (Informal Speech)　　　☛ Grammar 2

I Make informal question sentences using the cues and answer them in the negative.

Example (Will you) study Japanese today?

→　Q：今日、日本語を勉強する？　A：ううん、勉強しない。

1. (Do you) often ride a bus?

→　Q：＿＿＿＿＿＿＿＿＿＿＿　A：ううん、＿＿＿＿＿＿＿＿＿

2. (Do you) speak Japanese every day?

→　Q：＿＿＿＿＿＿＿＿＿＿＿　A：ううん、＿＿＿＿＿＿＿＿＿

3. (Do you) have homework today?

→　Q：＿＿＿＿＿＿＿＿＿＿＿　A：ううん、＿＿＿＿＿＿＿＿＿

4. (Will you) go out this weekend?

→　Q：＿＿＿＿＿＿＿＿＿＿＿　A：ううん、＿＿＿＿＿＿＿＿＿

5. Are you free tomorrow?

→　Q：＿＿＿＿＿＿＿＿＿＿＿　A：ううん、＿＿＿＿＿＿＿＿＿

6. Are you Japanese?

→　Q：＿＿＿＿＿＿＿＿＿＿＿　A：ううん、＿＿＿＿＿＿＿＿＿

7. Is it hot?

→　Q：＿＿＿＿＿＿＿＿＿＿＿　A：ううん、＿＿＿＿＿＿＿＿＿

II Answer the following questions in informal speech.

1. 今日は何曜日？

2. どんな食べ物がきらい？

3. 今週の週末、何をする？

第8課　3　Quotations（～と思います）　　　　　　☛Grammar 3

I Translate the following sentences. In sentences 4-6, "I don't think . . ." should be translated as ～ないと思います。

1. I think Professor Yamashita is good-looking.

2. I think this woman is Mary's Japanese teacher.

3. I think Professor Yamashita reads many books.

4. I don't think this town is interesting. (lit., I think this town is not interesting.)

5. I don't think Mai likes Mayumi.

6. I don't think it will snow tomorrow.

II Answer the following questions, using ～と思います。

1. あしたはどんな天気ですか。

2. 来週は忙しいですか。

3. あなたの日本語の先生は、料理が上手ですか。

4. あなたの日本語の先生は、今週の週末、何をしますか。

第8課　4　Quotations（〜と言っていました）　　　☛Grammar 4

▶ Ask someone (preferably Japanese) the following questions. Report the answers using 〜と言っていました.

Example　大学生ですか。→　田中さんは大学生だと言っていました。

1. 毎日、楽しいですか。

　　→

2. どんな果物が好きですか。

　　→

3. よくお酒を飲みますか。

　　→

4. どんなスポーツをよくしますか。

　　→

5. 兄弟がいますか。

　　→

6. どこに住んでいますか。

　　→

7. 結婚していますか。

　　→

8. 車を持っていますか。

　　→

9. 週末はたいてい何をしますか。

　　→

10. (your own question)

　　→

Get the signature of the person you interviewed: _____

第8課　5　～ないでください　　　　　　　　　　　　　☛Grammar 5

Ⅰ Translate the following sentences.

(Example)　Please don't wait for me. (Because) I will be late.

→　私を待たないでください。遅くなりますから。
　　わたし　ま　　　　　　　　　　　おそ

1. Please don't forget your umbrella. (Because) It will rain this afternoon.

→

2. Please don't open the window. (Because) I am cold.

→

3. Please don't turn off the TV. (Because) I'm watching the news (ニュース).

→

4. Please don't throw away the magazine. (Because) It's not my magazine.

→

Ⅱ Write the dictionary form of each of the verbs used in the following sentences.

(Example) たべないでください。　→　＿＿＿＿＿たべる＿＿＿＿＿

1. きらないでください。　　　＿＿＿＿＿＿＿＿＿＿＿＿

2. きないでください。　　　　＿＿＿＿＿＿＿＿＿＿＿＿

3. こないでください。　　　　＿＿＿＿＿＿＿＿＿＿＿＿

4. かかないでください。　　　＿＿＿＿＿＿＿＿＿＿＿＿

5. しないでください。　　　　＿＿＿＿＿＿＿＿＿＿＿＿

6. しなないでください。　　　＿＿＿＿＿＿＿＿＿＿＿＿

7. かえらないでください。　　＿＿＿＿＿＿＿＿＿＿＿＿

8. かわないでください。　　　＿＿＿＿＿＿＿＿＿＿＿＿

第8課　6　Verb のが好きです / 上手です

<small>す</small>　<small>じょうず</small>　　　　　　　　　　　　　☞ Grammar 6

I Write what you are good at/what you are not good at/what you like to do/what you don't like to do, using the verbs in the box.

speaking Japanese	driving a car	taking pictures	singing
listening to music	taking a bath	playing sports	cooking
doing laundry	cleaning	washing a car	

1. 私は＿＿＿＿＿＿＿＿＿＿＿＿＿＿＿＿下手です。
   <small>わたし</small>　　　　　　　　　　　　　　　　　<small>へ た</small>

2. 私は＿＿＿＿＿＿＿＿＿＿＿＿＿＿＿＿あまり上手じゃないです。
   <small>わたし</small>　　　　　　　　　　　　　　　　　　<small>じょうず</small>

3. 私は＿＿＿＿＿＿＿＿＿＿＿＿＿＿＿＿大好きです。
   <small>わたし</small>　　　　　　　　　　　　　　　　　<small>だい す</small>

4. 私は＿＿＿＿＿＿＿＿＿＿＿＿＿＿＿＿きらいです。
   <small>わたし</small>

5. 私は＿＿＿＿＿＿＿＿＿＿＿＿＿＿＿＿あまり好きじゃないです。
   <small>わたし</small>　　　　　　　　　　　　　　　　　　　<small>す</small>

II Translate the following sentences.

1. Erika is very good at making friends.

2. Kenta loves reading books.

3. Haruto hates cleaning the room.

4. Yui is not good at driving a car.

5. Yuki doesn't like doing laundry very much.

第8課　7　が・何か and 何も

☞Grammar 7・8

I Look at the picture of a party and complete the following conversations.

1. Q：だれが新聞を読んでいますか。

A：＿＿＿＿＿＿＿＿＿＿＿＿＿＿＿＿＿。

2. Q：＿＿＿＿＿＿＿＿＿＿＿＿＿＿＿＿＿。

A：森さんが撮っています。

3. Q：だれがめがねをかけていますか。

A：＿＿＿＿＿＿＿＿＿＿＿＿＿＿＿＿＿。

4. Q：＿＿＿＿＿＿＿＿＿＿＿＿＿＿＿＿＿。

A：田中さんがかぶっています。

II Translate the following sentences.

(Note especially that 何か and 何も are normally not accompanied by particles.)

1. Q：Did you eat anything this morning?

A：No, I did not eat anything this morning.

2. Q：What will you do over the weekend?

A：I won't do anything.

3. Would you like to drink something?

4. Kento asked something, but I did not understand.

第8課 8 答えましょう (Questions)
こた

Ⅰ Answer the following questions in Japanese using ～と思います.
おも

   1. 日本語のクラスについてどう思いますか。
に ほん ご　　　　　　　　　　　　おも

   2. 日本語の先生は何をするのが好きですか。
に ほん ご　せんせい　なに　　　　　　　　　す

   3. あした、雨が降りますか。
あめ　ふ

   4. あなたの友だちは料理が上手ですか。
とも　　　　りょう り　じょうず

Ⅱ Answer the following questions in Japanese.

   1. 何をするのが好きですか。
なに　　　　　　　す

   2. 何をするのが下手ですか。
なに　　　　　　　へ た

   3. 何をするのがきらいですか。
なに

   4. 掃除するのが好きですか。
そう じ　　　　　　す

第8課 9 聞く練習 (Listening Comprehension)

A Choose the picture that describes the situation in which you are likely to hear each of the sentences. 🔊 W08-A

1. (   )   2. (   )   3. (   )   4. (   )   5. (   )   6. (   )   7. (   )

(a)   (b)   (c)   (d)

(e)   (f)   (g)

B Robert and Ken are talking. Answer the questions in Japanese. 🔊 W08-B

＊〜と言っていた (casual version of 〜と言っていました)

1. ロバートさんとけんさんは、いつゲームをしますか。

2. たけしさんはゲームをしに来ますか。どうしてですか。

3. トムさんはゲームをしに来ますか。どうしてですか。

C Mary is reporting her interview with Professor Honma to the class. Circle every item that is true. 🔊 W08-C

＊インタビュー (interview)

1. On weekends, Professor Honma:

   [a. plays baseball   b. plays tennis   c. watches sports   d. goes on dates].

2. Professor Honma:

   [a. never cooks   b. cooks sometimes   c. is a good cook   d. is not a good cook].

3. Professor Honma's students are:

   [a. lively   b. quiet   c. diligent   d. kind   e. interesting].

第9課 1 Past Tense Short Forms   ☞Grammar 1

➤ Complete the chart below.

Verbs

dictionary form	past, affirmative	past, negative	long, present
e.g. たべる	たべた	たべなかった	たべます
1. よむ			
2. あそぶ			
3. おぼえる			
4. いく			
5. もらう			
6. おどる			
7. およぐ			
8. ひく			
9. やすむ			
10. する			
11. くる			

Adjectives/Noun

dictionary form	past, affirmative	past, negative
e.g. おもしろい	おもしろかった	おもしろくなかった
12. わかい		
13. かっこいい		
e.g. いじわる(な)	いじわるだった	いじわるじゃなかった
14. きれい(な)		
15. にちようび		

第9課　2　Past Tense Short Forms (Informal Speech)　　☞Grammar 2

I Make informal question sentences using the cues and answer them in the negative.

Example きのう、日本語を勉強する
にほんご べんきょう
→　Q：きのう、日本語を勉強した？　A：ううん、勉強しなかった。
にほんご べんきょう べんきょう

1. きのう、友だちに会う
とも あ
　→　Q：_____　A：ううん、_____

2. きのう、運動する
うんどう
　→　Q：_____　A：ううん、_____

3. 先週、試験がある
せんしゅう しけん
　→　Q：_____　A：ううん、_____

4. 先週の週末、大学に来る
せんしゅう しゅうまつ だいがく く
　→　Q：_____　A：ううん、_____

5. 先週の週末、楽しい
せんしゅう しゅうまつ たの
　→　Q：_____　A：ううん、_____

6. 子供の時、髪が長い
こども とき かみ なが
　→　Q：_____　A：ううん、_____

7. 子供の時、勉強がきらい
こども とき べんきょう
　→　Q：_____　A：ううん、_____

II Make your own questions you want to ask your friend about his/her childhood in informal speech.

Example 子供の時、よくスポーツをした？
こども とき

1.

2.

3.

第9課 3 Quotations （〜と思<small>おも</small>います） ☛Grammar 3

I Translate the following sentences, using the short form ＋ と思<small>おも</small>います. In sentences 4-6, "I don't think . . ." should be translated as 〜なかったと思<small>おも</small>います.

1. I think the concert began at nine o'clock.

2. I think Ken exercised last weekend.

3. I think Tadashi's father was good-looking when he was young.

4. I don't think last week's exam was difficult. (lit., I think last week's exam was not difficult.)

5. I don't think Mie was mean when she was a child.

6. I don't think Mai received a letter from Mari.

II Guess what your friends/family/teachers were like when they were children using 〜と思<small>おも</small>います.

Example メアリーさんは子供<small>こ ど も</small>の時<small>とき</small>、かわいかったと思<small>おも</small>います。

1.

2.

3.

第9課 4 Quotations (〜と言っていました)

🖝Grammar 4

▶ Ask someone (preferably Japanese) the following questions. Report the answers using 〜と言っていました.

Example 仕事は何ですか。 →　田中さんは会社員だと言っていました。

1. どんな音楽をよく聞きますか。

　→

2. 何をするのがきらいですか。

　→

3. 先週の週末、何をしましたか。

　→

4. 子供の時、いい子でしたか。

　→

5. 子供の時、背が高かったですか。

　→

6. 子供の時、学校が好きでしたか。

　→

7. 子供の時、どこに住んでいましたか。

　→

8. 子供の時、よく何をしましたか。

　→

9. (your own question)

　→

Get the signature of the person you interviewed: _____

第9課 5 Qualifying Nouns with Verbs ☞ Grammar 5

➤ Look at the picture and answer the questions. Use the pattern ○○さんは～ている人です,
describing what each person is currently doing.

1. みどりさんはどの人ですか。

2. ともやさんはどの人ですか。

3. はなさんはどの人ですか。

4. しんじさんはどの人ですか。

5. えりかさんはどの人ですか。

第9課 6 もう〜ました / まだ〜ていません　　　☞Grammar 6

▶ Write questions to ask if one has already done the things below. Answer the questions using もう or まだ. Pay attention to the verb forms in the affirmative and in the negative when you answer.

(Example) eat lunch

→　Q：もう昼ご飯を食べましたか。
　　　A：はい、もう食べました。／いいえ、まだ食べていません。

1. memorize new kanji

　　→　Q：_____

　　　　A：はい、_____

2. clean your room

　　→　Q：_____

　　　　A：いいえ、_____

3. talk with the new teacher

　　→　Q：_____

　　　　A：いいえ、_____

4. write a report

　　→　Q：_____

　　　　A：はい、_____

第9課　7　～から

☞ Grammar 7

Ⅰ　Translate the following sentences. Note that [the reason + から] precedes the result.

　　1. I won't exercise because I am sick today.

　　2. I will not take a walk today because it is raining.

　　3. Minami is very popular because she is good at dancing.

　　4. I was very lonely because I did not have any friends.

Ⅱ　Answer the questions, using [the short form + から].

　　Example　Q：きのう勉強しましたか。
　　　　　　 A：いいえ、宿題がなかったから、勉強しませんでした。

　　1. Q：先週は忙しかったですか。

　　　　A：＿＿＿＿＿＿＿＿＿＿＿＿＿＿＿＿＿＿＿＿＿＿＿＿＿＿＿。

　　2. Q：きのう、学校に来ましたか。

　　　　A：＿＿＿＿＿＿＿＿＿＿＿＿＿＿＿＿＿＿＿＿＿＿＿＿＿＿＿。

　　3. Q：今週の週末、出かけますか。

　　　　A：＿＿＿＿＿＿＿＿＿＿＿＿＿＿＿＿＿＿＿＿＿＿＿＿＿＿＿。

　　4. Q：来年も日本語を勉強しますか。

　　　　A：＿＿＿＿＿＿＿＿＿＿＿＿＿＿＿＿＿＿＿＿＿＿＿＿＿＿＿。

第9課　8　答えましょう (Questions)

▶ Answer the following questions in casual style.

1. きのうの晩ご飯は何を食べた？

　　おいしかった？

2. きのう何時ごろ寝た？

3. きのう洗濯した？

4. もう十課 (Lesson 10) の単語を覚えた？

5. 先週、映画を見た？

　　どうだった？

6. 子供の時、何をするのが好きだった？

7. 週末、何をした？

第9課 9 聞く練習 (Listening Comprehension)

A Ken and Yui are talking. Listen to the dialogue and answer the questions in Japanese.

🔊 W09-A ＊イタリア (Italy)

1. だれが遅くなりましたか。

2. けんさん／ゆいさんは何分ぐらい待ちましたか。

3. けんさんとゆいさんは何をしますか。

4. レストランはどこにありますか。

B Jun is showing the picture taken at his birthday party. Where are the following people in the picture? 🔊 W09-B

＊ケーキ (cake)　ワイン (wine)

1. (　　　) Jun
2. (　　　) Jun's friend
3. (　　　) Jun's younger sister
4. (　　　) Jun's older sister
5. (　　　) Jun's younger brother
6. (　　　) Jun's father
7. (　　　) Pochi

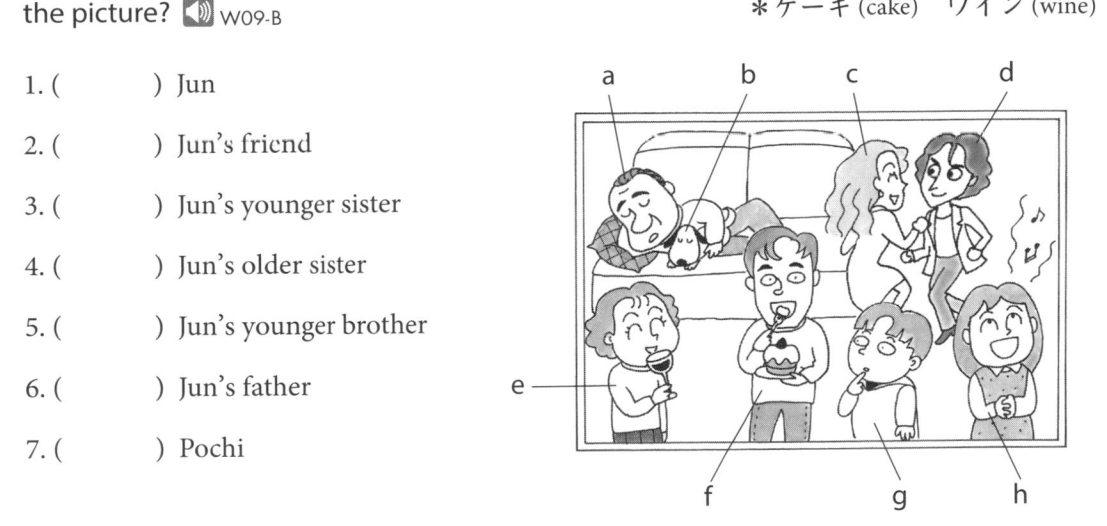

C Listen to the dialogue at a shop. How many of each item did the shopkeeper sell?

🔊 W09-C

How many?　Total amount

1. coffee　(　　　) ¥_____
2. orange　(　　　) ¥_____
　（オレンジ）
3. rice ball　(　　　) ¥_____
　（おにぎり）

4. tea　(　　　) ¥_____
5. boxed lunch　(　　　) ¥_____

第10課　1　Comparison between Two Items　　　　☛Grammar 1

I Translate the following sentences.

1. Russia (ロシア) is larger than Canada (カナダ).

2. Sundays are more fun than Mondays.

3. Takeshi is older than Mary.

4. Q：Which do you like better, soccer and baseball?

   A：I like baseball better.

II Make comparative sentences (both questions and answers).

(Example) Q：日本語のクラスとビジネスのクラスとどっちのほうが大変ですか。
　　　　　A：日本語のクラスのほうがビジネスのクラスより大変です。

1. Q：

   A：

2. Q：

   A：

第10課 2 Comparison among Three or More Items 👉Grammar 2

I Using the following categories, make "what/where/who is the most . . ." questions and answer them.

> **e.g.**
>
> | 日本料理 | 世界の町 | 有名人 | 季節 | 野菜 | 外国語 |
> |---|---|---|---|---|---|
> | に ほんりょう り | せ かい　まち | ゆうめいじん | き せつ | や さい | がいこく ご |

Example

Q：日本料理の中で、何がいちばんおいしいですか。
に ほんりょう り　なか　なに

A：すしがいちばんおいしいです。／すしがいちばんおいしいと思います。
おも

1. Q：

   A：

2. Q：

   A：

3. Q：

   A：

II Make comparison sentences with the items below.

Example　kanji / *katakana* / hiragana

→　漢字とカタカナとひらがなの中で、漢字がいちばん難しいです。
かん じ　　　　　　　　　　　　なか　　かん じ　　　　　　むずか

1. Takeshi / Robert / Professor Yamashita

2. meat / fish / vegetables

第10課　3　Adjective/Noun ＋ の

☞Grammar 3

I Look at the pictures and write your own answers, using の.

熱い (あつ)　　冷たい (つめ)

1. Q：どちらのコーヒーを飲(の)みますか。

A：＿＿＿＿＿＿＿＿＿＿＿＿＿＿＿＿＿＿＿＿＿＿。

きれい　　安い (やす)

2. Q：どちらのかばんがいいですか。

A：＿＿＿＿＿＿＿＿＿＿＿＿＿＿＿＿＿＿＿＿＿＿。

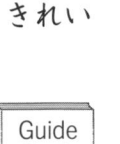

Guide Book Japan　ガイドブック日本

英語 (えいご)　　日本語 (にほんご)

3. Q：どちらのガイドブック (guidebook) を買(か)いますか。

A：＿＿＿＿＿＿＿＿＿＿＿＿＿＿＿＿＿＿＿＿＿＿。

II Translate the following sentences.

1. This clock is expensive. Give me a cheap one.

2. My computer is slower than yours.

3. What kind of movies do you like? —— I like scary ones.

4. This car is old. I will buy a new one.

5. This red T-shirt is more expensive than that white one.

第10課 4 〜つもりだ　　　　　　　　　　　☞Grammar 4

I Make sentences using 〜つもりです.

(Example)　see a movie tonight

→　今晩映画を見るつもりです。
こんばんえい が　　み

1. not go out on Sunday

→

2. work at a Japanese company

→

3. not get married

→

4. stay at my friend's house because hotels are expensive

→

II Answer the following questions, using 〜つもりです.

1. 今晩何をしますか。
こんばんなに

2. この週末、何をしますか。
しゅうまつ　　なに

3. 来年も日本語を勉強しますか。
らいねん　にほんご　べんきょう

4. 夏休み／冬休みに何をしますか。
なつやす　　ふゆやす　　なに

第10課　5　Adjective ＋ なる　　　　　　　　☛Grammar 5

Ⅰ Describe the following changes, using ～なりました.

1.
tall

2.

3.

1. _____

2. _____

3. _____

Ⅱ Translate the following sentences, using the verb なります. Pay attention to the order of elements in the sentences "(reason clause) から, (main clause)."

1. My room became clean, because I cleaned it this morning.

2. I have become sleepy, because I did not sleep much last night.

3. I have become very good at speaking Japanese, because I practiced a lot.

4. I will be (become) a teacher, because I like children.

第10課　6　どこかに / どこにも・〜で行きます　　　　☛Grammar 6・7

Ⅰ Translate the following sentences into Japanese.

1. Q：Are you going anywhere next holiday?

   A：No, I am not going anywhere.

2. Q：Did you do anything last weekend?

   A：No, I did not do anything.

3. Q：Did you meet anyone at the party?

   A：No, I did not meet anyone.

Ⅱ Based on the picture below, complete the following conversation.

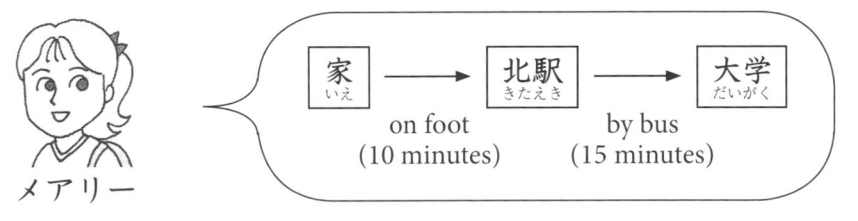

ゆい：　　　　メアリーさんは、家から北駅までどうやって行きますか。

メアリー：　1.＿＿＿＿＿＿＿＿＿＿＿＿＿＿＿＿＿。

ゆい：　　　そうですか。2.＿＿＿＿＿＿＿＿＿＿＿＿＿＿か。

メアリー：　十分かかります。

ゆい：　　　北駅から大学まで 3.＿＿＿＿＿＿＿＿＿＿＿＿＿＿か。

メアリー：　バスで行きます。

ゆい：　　　どのぐらいかかりますか。

メアリー：　そうですね、4.＿＿＿＿＿＿＿＿＿＿＿＿＿＿＿＿。

第10課　7　答えましょう (Questions)

▶ Answer the following questions in Japanese.

1. 食べ物の中で何がいちばん好きですか。

2. 季節の中でいつがいちばん好きですか。どうしてですか。

3. 有名人の中でだれがいちばん好きですか。どうしてですか。

4. あなたと日本語の先生とどっちのほうが背が高いですか。

5. あなたはどうやって家から学校まで行きますか。どのぐらいかかりますか。

6. 今度の休みにどこかに行きますか。

7. 先週の週末、何かしましたか。

8. 先週の週末、だれかに会いましたか。

第10課 8 聞く練習 (Listening Comprehension)

A Mary and her friends are talking about the upcoming winter vacation. Listen to the dialogue and fill in the chart in Japanese. 🔊 W10-A

	どこに 行きますか	何をしますか	どのぐらい 行きますか
メアリー			
ロバート			
たけし			
ソラ			

B Anita, who is a student at a Japanese language school, wants to go to college in Japan. She is interested in three universities (Hanaoka, Sakura, and Tsushima). Listen to the conversation between Anita and her Japanese teacher and answer the questions in Japanese. 🔊 W10-B　　　　　　　　＊学費 (tuition)

1. はなおか大学とさくら大学とつしま大学の中で、どれがいちばん大きいですか。

2. つしま大学の学費はいくらですか。

3. ここからさくら大学までどのぐらいかかりますか。どうやって行きますか。

4. どの大学の日本語のクラスがいちばんいいですか。

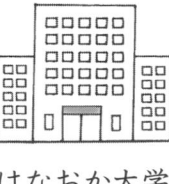
はなおか大学

さくら大学

つしま大学

C Read Yui's diary. Listen to the questions and write your answers in Japanese. 🔊 W10-C

冬休みに友だちと東京へ行った。12月11日にバスで行った。
東京で買い物をした。それから、東京ディズニーランドに
行った。12月15日に帰った。とても楽しかった。

---

1. _____

2. _____

3. _____

4. _____

5. _____

第11課　1　～たい　　　　　　　　　　　☛Grammar 1

Ⅰ　Choose from the list below two things you want to do and two things you don't want to do and make sentences.

山に登る	学校をやめる	うそをつく	ごろごろする	働く
旅行する	ピアノを習う	外国に住む	友だちとけんかする	

1.　What you want to do:

　(a)

　(b)

2.　What you don't want to do:

　(a)

　(b)

Ⅱ　Write whether you wanted or did not want to do the following things.

(Example)　go to school

　　　→　子供の時、学校に行きたかったです。／
　　　　　子供の時、学校に行きたくなかったです。

1.　own a dog

　　→

2.　eat snacks

　　→

3.　ride an airplane

　　→

4.　be a singer

　　→

5.　play games

　　→

第11課　2　〜たり〜たりする　　　　　　　　　　　　☞Grammar 2

I Translate the following sentences, using 〜たり〜たり. Pay attention to the sentence ending.

1. I watched a movie, shopped, etc., on the weekend.

2. I'll do laundry, study, etc., tomorrow.

3. I met a friend, read a book, etc., yesterday.

4. I practice Japanese, watch a Japanese movie, etc., at home.

5. I want to climb a mountain, go to a hot spring, etc., this weekend.

6. You must not smoke, drink beer, etc., at the dormitory (寮).

II Answer the questions, using 〜たり〜たり. Pay attention to the sentence ending.

1. デートの時、何をしますか。

2. 休みに何をしましたか。

3. 子供の時、よく何をしましたか。

4. 今度の週末、何がしたいですか。

第11課　3　〜ことがある

🖝Grammar 3

Ⅰ Choose from the list below three things you have done and three things you have never done and make sentences.

山に登る	英語を教える	地下鉄に乗る	日本料理を作る	働く
やま　のぼ	えい ご　おし	ち か てつ　の	に ほんりょう り　つく	はたら
猫を飼う	クラスで寝る	ピアノを習う	ダイエットをする	
ねこ　か	ね	なら		
温泉に入る	外国に住む	先生に手紙を書く	友だちとけんかする	
おんせん　はい	がいこく　す	せんせい　て がみ　か	とも	

---

1. What you have done:　　　　　　2. What you have never done:

(a)　　　　　　　　　　　　　　　　(a)

(b)　　　　　　　　　　　　　　　　(b)

(c)　　　　　　　　　　　　　　　　(c)

Ⅱ Make questions and answers using the cues.

(Example)　to tell a lie

→　Q：うそをついたことがありますか。

　　A：はい、あります。／いいえ、ありません。

1. to cut classes

　→　Q：

　　　A：

2. to climb Mt. Fuji（富士山）
　　　　　　　　　　　ふ じ さん

　→　Q：

　　　A：

第11課　4　Noun A や Noun B　　　☛Grammar 4

▶ Answer the questions with 〜や〜.

1. 大学の近くに何がありますか。
   <ruby>大学<rt>だいがく</rt></ruby>　<ruby>近<rt>ちか</rt></ruby>　<ruby>何<rt>なに</rt></ruby>

2. 今、十万円あります。何が買いたいですか。
   <ruby>今<rt>いま</rt></ruby>　<ruby>十万円<rt>じゅうまんえん</rt></ruby>　<ruby>何<rt>なに</rt></ruby>　<ruby>買<rt>か</rt></ruby>

3. 誕生日に何をもらいましたか。
   <ruby>誕生日<rt>たんじょうび</rt></ruby>　<ruby>何<rt>なに</rt></ruby>

4. 休みの日に、よくどこに行きますか。
   <ruby>休<rt>やす</rt></ruby>　<ruby>日<rt>ひ</rt></ruby>　<ruby>行<rt>い</rt></ruby>

5. 有名人の中で、だれに会いたいですか。
   <ruby>有名人<rt>ゆうめいじん</rt></ruby>　<ruby>中<rt>なか</rt></ruby>　<ruby>会<rt>あ</rt></ruby>

6. どんな日本料理を食べたことがありますか。
   <ruby>日本料理<rt>にほんりょうり</rt></ruby>　<ruby>食<rt>た</rt></ruby>

7. カラオケでどんな歌を歌いますか。
   <ruby>歌<rt>うた</rt></ruby>　<ruby>歌<rt>うた</rt></ruby>

第11課　5　答えましょう (Questions)

I Answer the following questions about your trip in Japanese.

1. どこに行きましたか。

2. そこで何をしましたか。(Use 〜たり〜たり.)

3. 食べ物はどうでしたか。何を食べましたか。(Use や.)

4. どんな所でしたか。(Use 〜て／〜で.)

5. また行きたいですか。どうしてですか。

II Answer the following questions in Japanese.

1. 子供の時、何になりたかったですか。

2. 今は何になりたいですか。どうしてですか。

3. 猫や犬を飼ったことがありますか。

第11課　6　聞く練習 (Listening Comprehension)
きくれんしゅう

A Ryota, Kana, and Ken are talking about their vacation. What did they do? What are they planning to do for the next vacation? Choose the answers from the list. ◀)) W11-A

＊ビーチ (beach)

a. skiing　　b. camping　　c. driving　　d. doing nothing	
e. shopping　　f. meeting friends　　g. taking a walk on a beach	
h. working part-time　　i. climbing mountains　　j. taking a spa bath	

	1. last vacation	2. next vacation
りょうた…	(　　) (　　)	(　　)
かな………	(　　) (　　) (　　)	(　　)
けん………	(　　)	(　　) (　　)

B Listen to the two short dialogues and choose the most appropriate answer(s). ◀)) W11-B

＊パンダ (panda)

Dialogue 1.　They are going to have [a. pizza　　b. sushi　　c. pasta (パスタ)].

Dialogue 2.　Where are they going to go in Tokyo?

Today:　　　[a. shopping　　b. art museum　　c. Kabuki　　d. zoo]

Tomorrow:　[a. shopping　　b. art museum　　c. Kabuki　　d. zoo]

C Listen to the dialogue and fill in the blanks. ◀)) W11-C

1. メアリーさんは、今、＿＿＿＿＿＿＿＿＿＿＿＿＿＿＿＿＿＿＿と言っていました。
いま　　　　　　　　　　　　　　　　　　　　　　　　　　　　　　　い

2. トムさんは、子供の時、＿＿＿＿＿＿＿＿＿＿＿＿＿＿＿＿＿＿と言っていました。
こども　とき　　　　　　　　　　　　　　　　　　　　　　　　い

3. 先生は、子供の時、＿＿＿＿＿＿＿＿＿＿＿＿＿＿＿＿＿＿＿と言っていました。
せんせい　こども　とき　　　　　　　　　　　　　　　　　　　　い

第12課 1 ～んです

🖝Grammar 1

Ⅰ Answer the question using ～んです according to the cues.

Q：どうしたんですか。

1. A：_____。
   (have a stomachache)

2. A：_____。
   (broke up with my girlfriend)

3. A：_____。
   (caught a cold)

4. A：_____。
   (have a hangover)

5. A：_____。
   (lost my train ticket)

6. A：_____。
   (got a bad grade)

Ⅱ Make up the reasons and answer the questions with ～んです.

1. Q：どうしてアルバイトをしているんですか。

   A：_____。

2. Q：どうしてきのう授業をサボったんですか。
         じゅぎょう

   A：_____。

3. Q：どうして疲れているんですか。
         つか

   A：_____。

4. Q：どうして緊張しているんですか。
         きんちょう

   A：_____。

第12課　2　〜すぎる

▶Grammar 2

I Complete the sentences according to the given cues.

1. このお菓子は＿＿＿＿＿＿＿＿＿＿＿＿＿＿＿＿＿＿＿＿＿＿＿＿＿＿＿。
　　　　　かし
　　　　　　　　　　　　　　　　　　　　(too sweet)

2. あの授業は＿＿＿＿＿＿＿＿＿＿＿＿＿＿＿＿＿＿＿＿＿＿＿＿＿＿＿。
　　　　　じゅぎょう
　　　　　　　　　　　　　　　　　　　(too difficult)

3. 今日は＿＿＿＿＿＿＿＿＿＿＿＿＿＿＿＿＿から、学校に行きたくないです。
　　　　きょう　　　　　(too cold)　　　　　　　　　　　　がっこう　い

4. 父は＿＿＿＿＿＿＿＿＿＿＿＿＿＿＿＿＿＿＿＿＿＿＿＿＿＿＿＿＿＿。
　　　ちち
　　　　　　　　　　　　　　　　　　(works too much)

5. ＿＿＿＿＿＿＿＿＿＿＿＿＿＿＿＿＿＿＿＿＿＿＿＿＿＿＿＿＿＿＿＿＿。
　　　　　　　　　　　(I often play games too much)

6. ＿＿＿＿＿＿＿＿＿＿＿＿＿＿＿＿＿＿＿＿＿から、頭が痛くなりました。
　　　　　　　　　　(was too nervous)　　　　　　　　　　あたま　いた

7. ＿＿＿＿＿＿＿＿＿＿＿＿＿＿＿＿＿＿から、のどが痛くなりました。
　　　　　　　　　(sang songs too much)　　　　　　　　　　　いた

8. 週末＿＿＿＿＿＿＿＿＿＿＿＿＿＿＿＿＿＿＿＿から、今日は勉強します。
　　しゅうまつ　　(played around too much)　　　　　　きょう　べんきょう

II Complain about something or somebody, using 〜すぎる.

Sample topics:　life / Japanese class / food in the cafeteria / your room / friend / father /

mother / teacher

1.

2.

第12課 3 〜ほうがいいです

☞Grammar 3

I Translate the following sentences.

1. You'd better go to a hospital.

2. You'd better memorize kanji.

3. You'd better call your mother more.

4. You'd better not worry.

5. You'd better not eat too much.

II Give advice using 〜ほうがいいですよ.

1. Your friend： あした試験があるんです。
   しけん

   You： _____。

2. Your friend： おなかがすいたんです。

   You： _____。

3. Your friend： かぜをひいたんです。

   You： _____。

第12課　4　〜ので

☛Grammar 4

I Translate the following sentences, using 〜ので. Note that [the reason+ので] precedes the result.

1. I got a bad grade because I didn't study.

2. I don't have money because I paid the electricity bill (fee).

3. I came to Japan because I wanted to study Japanese.

4. I don't want to do anything because I have a hangover.

5. I read the newspaper every day because I am interested in politics.

6. I will not go to the party tomorrow because I caught a cold.

II Answer the questions, using 〜ので.

(Example) Q：週末、何をするつもりですか。
　　　　　A：何も用事がないので、うちでごろごろするつもりです。

1. Q：歌手の中でだれが好きですか。

　　A：_____

2. Q：今どこにいちばん行きたいですか。

　　A：_____

3. Q：将来、どこに住みたいですか。

　　A：_____

第12課 5 ～なければいけません / ～なきゃいけません ☛Grammar 5

I Read the first half of the sentences. Then, choose what you have to do from the list and complete the sentences using ～なければいけません / ～なきゃいけません. You may use the same words *only* once.

| quit the part-time job | buy the textbook | do laundry | practice | get up early |

1. あしたは九時から授業があるので、＿＿＿＿＿＿＿＿＿＿＿＿＿＿＿＿＿＿＿＿。

2. 新しい授業が始まるので、＿＿＿＿＿＿＿＿＿＿＿＿＿＿＿＿＿＿＿＿＿＿。

3. 来週サッカーの試合があるので、＿＿＿＿＿＿＿＿＿＿＿＿＿＿＿＿＿＿＿＿。

4. お母さんが病気なので、＿＿＿＿＿＿＿＿＿＿＿＿＿＿＿＿＿＿＿＿＿＿＿＿。

5. 勉強が忙しくなったので、＿＿＿＿＿＿ ＿＿＿＿ ＿＿＿＿＿＿＿＿＿＿＿。

II Write two things you have to do this week and two things you had to do yesterday.

1. This week:

(a)

(b)

2. Yesterday:

(a)

(b)

第12課　6　〜でしょうか　　　　　☛Grammar 6

▶ You live in a dormitory and you will get a new roommate. Ask the coordinator what that person is like, using 〜でしょうか.

1. Is she/he Japanese?

2. What is her/his major?

3. Is she/he a quiet person?

4. What kind of music does she/he like?

5. Does she/he smoke?

6. Does she/he have many friends?

7. (your own question)

8. (your own question)

第12課　7　答えましょう (Questions)

▶ Answer the following questions in Japanese.

1. アレルギーがありますか。何のアレルギーですか。

2. よく何をしすぎますか。

3. 今、何に興味がありますか。

4. 日本語のクラスは宿題が多いと思いますか。

5. 悪い成績を取ったことがありますか。

6. かぜの時、何をしないほうがいいですか。

7. 今週の週末、何をしなければいけませんか。

第12課 8 聞く練習 (Listening Comprehension)

A Listen to the three dialogues at the health clinic. Mark ◯ for the symptoms each patient has and write down the doctor's suggestion in Japanese. 🔊 W12-A

＊さしみ (raw fish)　ねつをはかる (take one's temperature)

Patient	sore throat	head-ache	stomach-ache	cough	fever	doctor's suggestion
1						
2						
3						

B Two colleagues are talking at the office. Listen to the dialogue and answer the following questions in Japanese. 🔊 W12-B

1. 男の人は今晩飲みに行きますか。どうしてですか。

2. 男の人はもうプレゼントを買いましたか。

C A student will study in Japan. Listen to the conversation at the study abroad counselor's office. Mark each of the following statements with ◯ if true, or with ✕ if false. 🔊 W12-C

＊寮 (dormitory)

1. (　　　　) The student wants a Japanese roommate.

2. (　　　　) It takes 30 minutes from the dormitory to the university by bicycle.

3. (　　　　) There is a bath in each room.

読み書き編

よ か へん

Reading and Writing

第1課　1　*Hiragana*（あ – こ）

Ⅰ Practice writing the following ten *hiragana* (あ through こ).

a	あ	ー　十 あ	あ	あ	あ				
i	い	い　い	い	い	い				
u	う	丶　う	う	う	う				
e	え	丶　え	え	え	え				
o	お	ー　お お	お	お	お				
ka	か	つ　カ か	か	か	か				
ki	き	ー　二 キ　き	き	き	き				
ku	く	く	く	く	く				
ke	け	し　に け	け	け	け				
ko	こ	ー　こ	こ	こ	こ				

Ⅱ Choose the right romanization for each of the *hiragana* words below.

1. こい (　　) (carp)
2. うえ (　　) (above)
3. おか (　　) (hill)
4. あき (　　) (autumn)
5. いけ (　　) (pond)
6. かく (　　) (write)

a. *kaku*	d. *ike*
b. *aki*	e. *koi*
c. *ue*	f. *oka*

Ⅲ Write the words below in *hiragana*.

1. *au* (meet)
2. *ie* (house)
3. *ai* (love)
4. *kao* (face)
5. *koe* (voice)
6. *kiku* (listen)

第1課　2　*Hiragana* (さ – と)
だい いっ か

I Practice writing the following ten *hiragana* (さ through と).

sa	さ	ー ＊／さ	さ	さ	さ				
shi	し	し	し	し	し				
su	す	ー／す	す	す	す				
se	せ	ー ＋／せ	せ	せ	せ				
so	そ	そ	そ	そ	そ				
ta	た	ー ナ／たー た	た	た	た				
chi	ち	ー ち	ち	ち	ち				
tsu	つ	つ	つ	つ	つ				
te	て	て	て	て	て				
to	と	ヽ と	と	と	と				

II Choose the right romanization for each of the *hiragana* words below.

1. あさ (　) (morning)
2. とち (　) (land)
3. かたて (　) (one hand)
4. すし (　) (sushi)
5. きせつ (　) (season)
6. そと (　) (outside)

a. *kisetsu*	d. *tochi*
b. *soto*	e. *sushi*
c. *katate*	f. *asa*

III Write the words below in *hiragana*.

1. *tasuke* (help)
2. *chikatetsu* (subway)
3. *sekai* (world)
4. *kasa* (umbrella)
5. *toshi* (age)
6. *asoko* (over there)

第1課 3 *Hiragana*（な – ほ）

I Practice writing the following ten *hiragana*（な through ほ）.

na	な	— ナ / ナ な	な	な	な				
ni	に	し に / に	に	に	に				
nu	ぬ	＼ ぬ	ぬ	ぬ	ぬ				
ne	ね	し ね	ね	ね	ね				
no	の	の	の	の	の				
ha	は	し に / は	は	は	は				
hi	ひ	ひ	ひ	ひ	ひ				
fu	ふ	、 ふ / ふ ふ	ふ	ふ	ふ				
he	へ	へ	へ	へ	へ				
ho	ほ	し に / に ほ	ほ	ほ	ほ				

II Choose the right romanization for each of the *hiragana* words below.

1. ひふ（   ）
   (skin)
2. なにか（   ）
   (something)
3. ほね（   ）
   (bone)
4. しぬ（   ）
   (die)
5. このは（   ）
   (leaf)
6. へた（   ）
   (clumsy)

a. *shinu*	d. *hifu*
b. *hone*	e. *heta*
c. *nanika*	f. *konoha*

III Write the words below in *hiragana*.

1. *fune*
   (boat)
2. *hoshi*
   (star)
3. *hana*
   (flower)
4. *heso*
   (navel)
5. *nuno*
   (cloth)
6. *hiniku*
   (sarcasm)

第1課 4 *Hiragana* (ま – よ)

I Practice writing the following eight *hiragana* (ま through よ).

ma	ま	一 / ニ / ま	ま	ま	ま				
mi	み	み / み	み	み	み				
mu	む	ー / む / む	む	む	む				
me	め	＼ / め	め	め	め				
mo	も	し / も / も	も	も	も				
ya	や	っ / ゃ / や	や	や	や				
yu	ゆ	わ / ゆ	ゆ	ゆ	ゆ				
yo	よ	ー / よ	よ	よ	よ				

II Choose the right romanization for each of the *hiragana* words below.

1. まち (   )
   (town)

2. みせ (   )
   (store)

3. むね (   )
   (chest)

4. ゆめ (   )
   (dream)

5. もや (   )
   (fog)

6. よむ (   )
   (read)

a. *mune*	d. *yomu*
b. *mise*	e. *yume*
c. *moya*	f. *machi*

III Write the words below in *hiragana*.

1. *mochi*
   (rice cake)

2. *matsu*
   (wait)

3. *kami*
   (paper; hair)

4. *oyu*
   (hot water)

5. *musume*
   (daughter)

6. *yoyaku*
   (reservation)

第1課 5 *Hiragana* (ら‐ん)

I Practice writing the following eight *hiragana* (ら through ん).

ra ら	`	ら	ら	ら	ら			
ri り	l	り	り	り	り			
ru る	る		る	る	る			
re れ	l	れ	れ	れ	れ			
ro ろ	ろ		ろ	ろ	ろ			
wa わ	l	わ	わ	わ	わ			
o (wo) を	一	を	を	を	を			
	一 を							
n ん	ん		ん	ん	ん			

II Choose the right romanization for each of the *hiragana* words below.

1. わらう (   )
   (laugh)

2. よる (   )
   (night)

3. きいろ (   )
   (yellow)

4. はれ (   )
   (sunny)

5. きをつけて (   )
   (Watch out!)

6. しんり (   )
   (psychology)

a. *yoru*	e. *warau*
b. *shinri*	f. *kiiro*
c. *hare*	
d. *ki o/wo tsukete*	

III Write the words below in *hiragana*.

1. *wakaru*
   (understand)

2. *rekishi*
   (history)

3. *me o(=wo) samasu*
   (wake up)

4. *riron*
   (theory)

5. *rainen*
   (next year)

6. *han ei*
   (prosperity)

第1課　6　*Hiragana* (Dots/Circles/Small や, ゆ, よ)

I Listen to the recording and choose the correct *hiragana* word. 🔊 WY-1

1. a. かき
   b. かぎ
2. a. ぶんか
   b. ふんか
3. a. にんしん
   b. にんじん
4. a. けんぽう
   b. けんぼう

II Listen to the recording carefully and fill in the boxes with *hiragana*. 🔊 WY-2

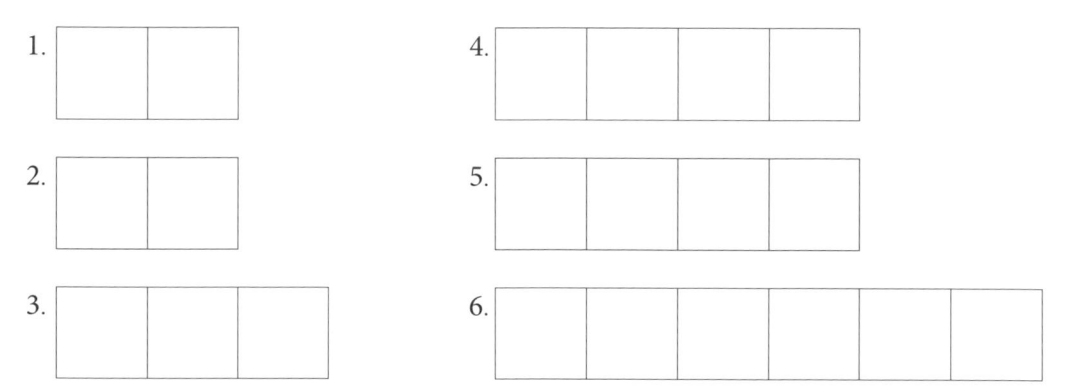

1. ☐☐
4. ☐☐☐

2. ☐☐
5. ☐☐☐

3. ☐☐
6. ☐☐☐☐

III Listen to the recording and choose the correct *hiragana* word. 🔊 WY-3

1. a. しょみ
   b. しゅみ
2. a. じんじゃ
   b. じんじょ
3. a. りよかん
   b. りょかん
4. a. きやく
   b. きゃく

IV Listen to the recording and fill in the boxes with *hiragana*. 🔊 WY-4

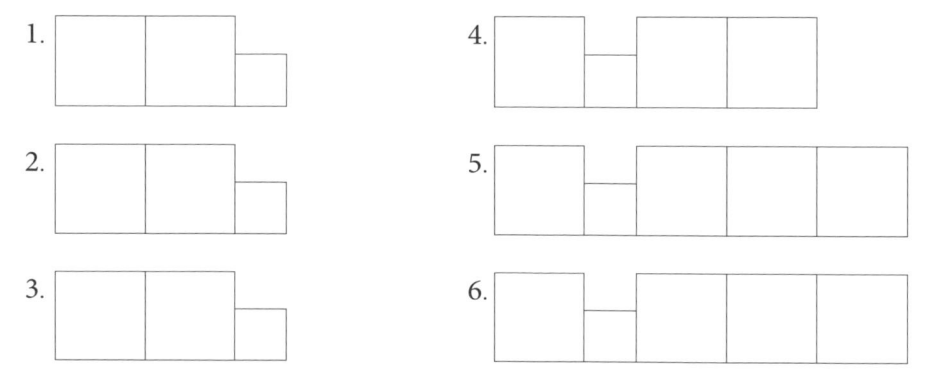

1. ☐☐☐
4. ☐☐☐

2. ☐☐☐
5. ☐☐☐☐

3. ☐☐☐
6. ☐☐☐

第1課 だい いっ か　7　*Hiragana* (Double Consonants/Long Vowels)

I Listen to the recording and choose the correct *hiragana* word. 🔊 WY-5

1. ⎰ a. さか
   ⎱ b. さっか

2. ⎰ a. いっさい
   ⎱ b. いさい

3. ⎰ a. あない
   ⎱ b. あんない

4. ⎰ a. ざっし
   ⎱ b. ざし

II Listen to the recording carefully and fill in the boxes with *hiragana*. 🔊 WY-6

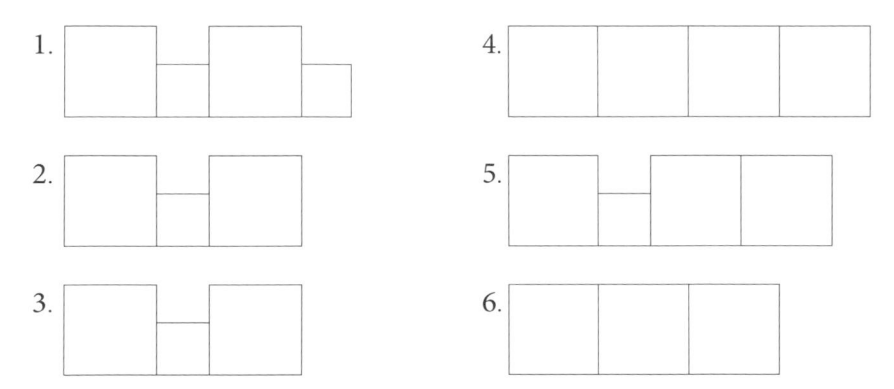

1. ☐☐☐

4. ☐☐☐☐

2. ☐☐☐

5. ☐☐☐

3. ☐☐☐

6. ☐☐

III Listen to the recording and choose the correct *hiragana* word. 🔊 WY-7

1. ⎰ a. おじさん
   ⎱ b. おじいさん

2. ⎰ a. さよなら
   ⎱ b. さようなら

3. ⎰ a. えいが
   ⎱ b. えが

4. ⎰ a. くうき
   ⎱ b. くき

IV Listen to the recording and fill in the boxes with *hiragana*. 🔊 WY-8

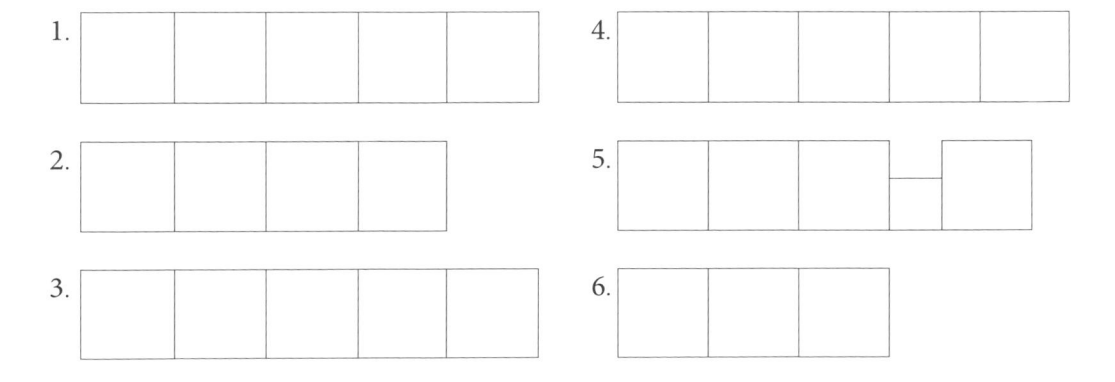

1. ☐☐☐☐

4. ☐☐☐☐

2. ☐☐☐

5. ☐☐☐☐

3. ☐☐☐☐

6. ☐☐

第2課 だいにか 1 *Katakana* (ア－コ)

Ⅰ Practice writing the following ten *katakana* (ア through コ).

a	ア	⁻ ア	ア	ア	ア				
i	イ	ノ イ	イ	イ	イ				
u	ウ	' '' ウ	ウ	ウ	ウ				
e	エ	⁻ ⊤ エ	エ	エ	エ				
o	オ	⁻ ナ オ	オ	オ	オ				
ka	カ	フ カ	カ	カ	カ				
ki	キ	⁻ ニ キ	キ	キ	キ				
ku	ク	ノ ク	ク	ク	ク				
ke	ケ	ノ ヒ ケ	ケ	ケ	ケ				
ko	コ	フ コ	コ	コ	コ				

Ⅱ Write the words below in *katakana*.

Unlike the *hiragana* writing system, long vowels in *katakana* words are transcribed with a bar. For example: リー (りい in *hiragana*), カー (かあ in *hiragana*).

1. おーけー
   (okay)

2. けーき
   (cake)

3. うえあ
   (wear)

4. こーく
   (Coke)

5. きうい
   (kiwifruit)

6. ここあ
   (cocoa)

第2課　2　*Katakana*（サ–ト）

I Practice writing the following ten *katakana* (サ through ト).

sa	サ	一　ナ / サ	サ	サ	サ					
shi	シ	丶　丶゛/ シ	シ	シ	シ					
su	ス	フ　ス	ス	ス	ス					
se	セ	一　セ	セ	セ	セ					
so	ソ	丶　ソ	ソ	ソ	ソ					
ta	タ	ノ　ク / タ	タ	タ	タ					
chi	チ	ノ　二 / チ	チ	チ	チ					
tsu	ツ	丶　丶゛/ ツ	ツ	ツ	ツ					
te	テ	一　二 / テ	テ	テ	テ					
to	ト	｜　ト	ト	ト	ト					

II Write the words below in *katakana*.

1. しーざー
   (Caesar)

2. すーつ
   (suit)

3. せっと
   (set)

4. そっくす
   (socks)

5. たこす
   (tacos)

6. ちーず
   (cheese)

7. たい
   (Thailand)

8. でっき
   (deck)

第2課　3　*Katakana*（ナ－ホ）

Ⅰ Practice writing the following ten *katakana* (ナ through ホ).

na	ナ	ー ナ	ナ	ナ	ナ					
ni	二	‐ 二	二	二	二					
nu	ヌ	フ ヌ	ヌ	ヌ	ヌ					
ne	ネ	、 ヲ / ネ ヲ ネ	ネ	ネ	ネ					
no	ノ	ノ	ノ	ノ	ノ					
ha	ハ	ノ ハ	ハ	ハ	ハ					
hi	ヒ	‐ ヒ	ヒ	ヒ	ヒ					
fu	フ	フ	フ	フ	フ					
he	ヘ	ヘ	ヘ	ヘ	ヘ					
ho	ホ	‐ ナ / オ ホ	ホ	ホ	ホ					

Ⅱ Write the words below in *katakana*.

1. ぼさのば
(bossa nova)

2. かぬー
(canoe)

3. はーぶ
(herb)

4. びきに
(bikini)

5. なっつ
(nuts)

6. ぺっと
(pet)

7. こね
(connection)

8. はっぴー
(happy)

9. ねくたい
(necktie)

10. のーと
(notebook)

第2課　4　*Katakana*（マ – ヨ）

I Practice writing the following eight *katakana*（マ through ヨ）.

ma	マ	フ／マ	マ	マ	マ						
mi	ミ	｀／ニ／ミ	ミ	ミ	ミ						
mu	ム	∠／ム	ム	ム	ム						
me	メ	ノ／メ	メ	メ	メ						
mo	モ	一／二／モ	モ	モ	モ						
ya	ヤ	一／ヤ	ヤ	ヤ	ヤ						
yu	ユ	フ／ユ	ユ	ユ	ユ						
yo	ヨ	フ／ヨ／ヨ	ヨ	ヨ	ヨ						

II Write the words below in *katakana*.

1. めも
   (memo)

2. むーど
   (mood)

3. みに
   (mini)

4. まや
   (Maya)

5. よっと
   (yacht)

6. ゆーざー
   (user)

7. きゃっぷ
   (cap)

8. しちゅー
   (stew)

9. しょっく
   (shock)

10. はーもにか
    (harmonica)

第2課　5　*Katakana* （ラ－ン）

I Practice writing the following eight *katakana* （ラ through ン）.

ra	ラ	ˉ　ラ	ラ	ラ	ラ			
ri	リ	ˈ　リ	リ	リ	リ			
ru	ル	ノ　ル	ル	ル	ル			
re	レ	レ	レ	レ	レ			
ro	ロ	ˈ　ロ / ロ	ロ	ロ	ロ			
wa	ワ	ˈ　ワ	ワ	ワ	ワ			
o (wo)	ヲ	ˉ　＝ / ヲ	ヲ	ヲ	ヲ			
n	ン	丶　ン	ン	ン	ン			

II Write the words below in *katakana*.

The small *katakana* エ is used with シ and チ to transcribe the sounds "she" and "che": シェパード (shepherd) and チェック (check), for example.

1. よーろっぱ
   (Europe)

2. わっくす
   (wax)

3. るーれっと
   (roulette)

4. あふりか
   (Africa)

5. らーめん
   (ramen noodles)

6. しぇーくすぴあ
   (Shakespeare)

7. ちぇっくいん
   (check-in)

8 よーぐると
   (yogurt)

第3課 | 1 | Kanji Practice

001	一	一	一	一				
002	二	二	二	二				
003	三	三	三	三				
004	四	四	四	四				
005	五	五	五	五				
006	六	六	六	六				
007	七	七	七	七				
008	八	八	八	八				
009	九	九	九	九				
010	十	十	十	十				
011	百	百	百	百				
012	千	千	千	千				
013	万	万	万	万				
014	円	円	円	円				
015	時	時	時	時				

第3課　2　Using Kanji

I Write the numbers in kanji.

1. 41

2. 300

3. 1,500

4. 2,890

5. 10,000

6. 67,000

7. 128,000

8. 1,000,000

Ⅱ Write in kanji.

1. A：これはいくらですか。　　B：＿＿＿＿＿＿＿＿です。
　　　　　　　　　　　　　　　　　　　ろっぴゃくえん

2. A：いまなん＿＿＿＿ですか。　B：＿＿＿＿＿＿です。
　　　　　　　　　じ　　　　　　　　　　　よじ

Ⅲ Using the kanji you know, translate the sentences into Japanese.

1. This watch is 49,000 yen.

2. That bag is 5,300 yen.

3. Ms. Yamanaka gets up at six.

4. Ms. Kawaguchi goes to college at seven.

5. Mr. Suzuki usually goes to bed at about twelve.

6. I sometimes drink coffee at a cafe. The coffee is 380 yen.

第4課　1　Kanji Practice

016 日	日	日	日					
017 本	本	本	本					
018 人	人	人	人					
019 月	月	月	月					
020 火	火	火	火					
021 水	水	水	水					
022 木	木	木	木					
023 金	金	金	金					
024 土	土	土	土					
025 曜	曜	曜	曜					
026 上	上	上	上					
027 下	下	下	下					
028 中	中	中	中					
029 半	半	半	半					

第4課　2　Using Kanji

Ⅰ Write kanji and their readings for the following words as shown in the example.

Example　Sunday　　　日 曜 日
　　　　　　　　　　　（　にちようび　）

1. Monday　　　＿＿＿＿＿＿＿
　　　　　　　（　　　　　　　）

4. Thursday　　　＿＿＿＿＿＿＿
　　　　　　　　（　　　　　　　）

2. Tuesday　　　＿＿＿＿＿＿＿
　　　　　　　（　　　　　　　）

5. Friday　　　＿＿＿＿＿＿＿
　　　　　　　（　　　　　　　）

3. Wednesday　　　＿＿＿＿＿＿＿
　　　　　　　　（　　　　　　　）

6. Saturday　　　＿＿＿＿＿＿＿
　　　　　　　　（　　　　　　　）

Ⅱ Write in kanji.

1. ＿＿＿＿＿ご の ＿＿＿＿ は かばんの ＿＿＿＿ です。　　2. ＿＿＿＿ をのみます。
　　にほん　　　　　ほん　　　　　　　　なか　　　　　　　　　　　　みず

3. いま、＿＿＿＿＿＿＿ です。　　　4. あの ＿＿＿＿ はだれですか。
　　　　　　ろくじはん　　　　　　　　　　　ひと

5. エレベーター (elevator) は ＿＿＿＿ にいきますか。＿＿＿＿ にいきますか。
　　　　　　　　　　　　　　うえ　　　　　　　　　　した

6. わたしのともだちは ＿＿＿＿＿＿＿ です。
　　　　　　　　　　にほんじん

Ⅲ Using the kanji you know, translate the sentences into Japanese.

1. I went to a restaurant with a Japanese friend on Friday.

2. I got up at about ten-thirty on Saturday.

3. I went to a temple alone in January.

第5課　1　Kanji Practice

030 山	山	山	山						
031 川	川	川	川						
032 元	元	元	元						
033 気	気	気	気						
034 天	天	天	天						
035 私	私	私	私						
036 今	今	今	今						
037 田	田	田	田						
038 女	女	女	女						
039 男	男	男	男						
040 見	見	見	見						
041 行	行	行	行						
042 食	食	食	食						
043 飲	飲	飲	飲						

第5課 2 Using Kanji

I Write the appropriate mixes of kanji and *hiragana*.

1. _____ですか。
   げんき

2. _____はいい_____ですね。
   きょう   てんき

3. あの_____の_____は_____さんです。
   おとこ   ひと   やまかわ

4. あの_____の_____は_____さんです。
   おんな   ひと   やまだ

5. _____はきのう_____に_____。
   わたし   かわ   いきました

6. ピザを_____。 コーヒーを_____。
   たべました   のみました

7. うちでテレビを_____。
   みました

II Using the kanji you know, translate the sentences into Japanese.

1. I am now in Japan.

2. Ms. Tanaka is fine. Mr. Yamakawa is not fine.

3. I went to the mountain with a Japanese man and woman.

4. I drank coffee with my friend on Tuesday.

5. On Wednesday, I ate dinner at home. And then I watched TV.

第6課　1　Kanji Practice

044	東	東	東	東					
045	西	西	西	西					
046	南	南	南	南					
047	北	北	北	北					
048	口	口	口	口					
049	出	出	出	出					
050	右	右	右	右					
051	左	左	左	左					
052	分	分	分	分					
053	先	先	先	先					
054	生	生	生	生					
055	大	大	大	大					
056	学	学	学	学					
057	外	外	外	外					
058	国	国	国	国					

第6課 2 Using Kanji

I Write the appropriate mixes of kanji and *hiragana*.

1. _____ _____ _____ _____
　　ひがし　　にし　　みなみ　　きた

2. きのう_____。
　　　　　　　　でかけました

3. _____を_____、_____へ_____行ってください。
　　みなみぐち　　　　でて　　　　みぎ　　ごふん

4. _____を_____、_____へ_____行ってください。
　　にしぐち　　　　でて　　　ひだり　じゅっぷん

5. チョウさんは_____です。_____からきました。
　　　　　　　　だいがくせい　　　　　　ちゅうごく

6. _____はよく_____と_____に行きます。
　　せんせい　　　　がくせい　　　がいこく

II Using the kanji you know, translate the sentences into Japanese.

1. There are lots of foreign teachers at my college.

2. The college is to the left of a bank.

3. Go out the east exit and go to the right, please.

4. Where is the exit?

5. I waited for twenty minutes at the north exit.

第7課 1 Kanji Practice

059 京	京	京	京				
060 子	子	子	子				
061 小	小	小	小				
062 会	会	会	会				
063 社	社	社	社				
064 父	父	父	父				
065 母	母	母	母				
066 高	高	高	高				
067 校	校	校	校				
068 毎	毎	毎	毎				
069 語	語	語	語				
070 文	文	文	文				
071 帰	帰	帰	帰				
072 入	入	入	入				

第7課　2　Using Kanji

I Write the appropriate mixes of kanji and *hiragana*.

1. ＿＿＿＿＿で＿＿＿＿さんの＿＿＿＿＿＿に＿＿＿＿＿＿＿＿。
   とうきょう　　きょうこ　　　　　　おとうさん　　　　　あいました

2. ＿＿＿と＿＿は＿＿＿＿、＿＿＿＿に行きます。
   ちち　　はは　　まいにち　　かいしゃ

3. ＿＿＿＿は八時に＿＿＿＿に行って、五時に家に＿＿＿＿＿＿＿＿。
   こども　　　　がっこう　　　　　　　　いえ　　　かえりました

4. このケーキは＿＿＿＿＿＿、＿＿＿＿です。
   ちいさくて　　　たかい

5. サークルに＿＿＿＿＿＿＿います。
   はいって

6. ＿＿＿＿＿で＿＿＿＿＿＿と＿＿＿＿を勉強しました。
   こうこう　　　にほんご　　　ぶんがく　　べんきょう

II Using the kanji you know, translate the sentences into Japanese.

1. Kyoko's younger sister is a high school student.

2. Kyoko's mother works at a small company.

3. My father comes home late every day.

4. I am studying Japanese and literature.

5. Ms. Minami speaks English a little.

第8課　1　Kanji Practice

073 員	員	員	員					
074 新	新	新	新					
075 聞	聞	聞	聞					
076 作	作	作	作					
077 仕	仕	仕	仕					
078 事	事	事	事					
079 電	電	電	電					
080 車	車	車	車					
081 休	休	休	休					
082 言	言	言	言					
083 読	読	読	読					
084 思	思	思	思					
085 次	次	次	次					
086 何	何	何	何					

第8課 2 Using Kanji

I Write the appropriate mixes of kanji and *hiragana*.

1. 川口さんは＿＿＿＿＿＿＿＿＿だと＿＿＿＿＿＿＿＿＿。
   かわぐち　　　　　かいしゃいん　　　　　　　おもいます

2. 友だちは＿＿＿＿＿を＿＿＿＿＿と＿＿＿＿＿＿＿いました。
   とも　　　　しごと　　　やすむ　　　　いって

3. ＿＿＿＿＿を＿＿＿＿＿＿＿。
   しんぶん　　　よみます

4. ＿＿＿＿＿＿＿＿＿ ＿＿＿＿＿を買いました。
   あたらしい　　　　くるま　　　か

5. ＿＿＿の＿＿＿＿＿は＿＿＿＿＿ですか。
   つぎ　　でんしゃ　　　なんじ

6. ＿＿＿＿＿の日にピザを＿＿＿＿＿＿＿＿＿＿＿。
   やすみ　　　　　　　　　つくりました

II Using the kanji you know, translate the sentences into Japanese.

1. I listen to music on the train.

2. Please turn on the light.

3. I think company employees in Japan are busy.

4. What do you do on holidays?

5. My mother said that she would go to Tokyo next week.

6. The next train comes at eleven o'clock.

第9課 1 Kanji Practice

087 午	午	午	午				
088 後	後	後	後				
089 前	前	前	前				
090 名	名	名	名				
091 白	白	白	白				
092 雨	雨	雨	雨				
093 書	書	書	書				
094 友	友	友	友				
095 間	間	間	間				
096 家	家	家	家				
097 話	話	話	話				
098 少	少	少	少				
099 古	古	古	古				
100 知	知	知	知				
101 来	来	来	来				

第9課 2 Using Kanji

I Write the appropriate mixes of kanji and *hiragana*.

1. ＿＿＿＿＿＿＿＿は＿＿＿＿が降っていました。
   ごぜんちゅう　　　あめ　　ふ

2. ＿＿＿＿＿は＿＿＿＿＿＿の＿＿＿に行って、＿＿＿＿＿＿＿＿＿＿。
   ごご　　　　ともだち　　　いえ　　　　　　はなしました

3. この＿＿＿＿＿着物は＿＿＿＿＿ ＿＿＿＿＿です。
   しろい　きもの　　すこし　　ふるい

4. あの人の＿＿＿＿＿を＿＿＿＿＿＿いますか。＿＿＿＿＿＿ください。
   なまえ　　　　しって　　　　　　かいて

5. ＿＿＿＿＿＿＿待ちましたが、スーさんは＿＿＿＿＿＿＿＿＿＿＿＿。
   にじかん　ま　　　　　　　　　　きませんでした

6. 今、＿＿＿＿＿がないから、クラスの＿＿＿、＿＿＿をしましょう。
   じかん　　　　　　　　　あと　　はなし

II Using the kanji you know, translate the sentences into Japanese.

1. I wrote a letter to my friend in the afternoon.

2. I read a book for one hour at home.

3. The post office is between the bank and the bookstore.

4. My friend is behind the teacher.

5. The bus stop is in front of the university.

6. I will call you later.

第10課　1　Kanji Practice

102　住	住	住	住					
103　正	正	正	正					
104　年	年	年	年					
105　売	売	売	売					
106　買	買	買	買					
107　町	町	町	町					
108　長	長	長	長					
109　道	道	道	道					
110　雪	雪	雪	雪					
111　立	立	立	立					
112　自	自	自	自					
113　夜	夜	夜	夜					
114　朝	朝	朝	朝					
115　持	持	持	持					

第10課 2 Using Kanji

I Write the appropriate mixes of kanji and *hiragana*.

1. ＿＿＿＿＿、この＿＿＿に＿＿＿＿つもりです。
   らいねん　　　　まち　　　すむ

2. ＿＿＿＿＿の＿＿＿＿＿＿に＿＿＿が降りました。
   ことし　　　おしょうがつ　　ゆき　ふ

3. ＿＿＿＿の時計を＿＿＿＿、友だちのプレゼントを＿＿＿＿＿＿。
   じぶん　　とけい　　うって　　　　　　　　　かいました

4. ＿＿＿におじぞうさんが＿＿＿＿＿＿います。
   みち　　　　　　　　　たって

5. あしたの＿＿＿、かさを＿＿＿＿＿＿きてください。
   あさ　　　　　もって

6. ＿＿＿が＿＿＿＿なりました。
   よる　　　ながく

II Using the kanji you know, translate the sentences into Japanese.

1. I will become a third-year student this year.

2. It snowed this morning.

3. I sold my old car and bought a new one.

4. Ms. Yamada is tall and has long hair.

5. Shall I carry your bag?

6. A new year will begin tomorrow.

第11課 1 Kanji Practice

116	手	手	手	手					
117	紙	紙	紙	紙					
118	好	好	好	好					
119	近	近	近	近					
120	明	明	明	明					
121	病	病	病	病					
122	院	院	院	院					
123	映	映	映	映					
124	画	画	画	画					
125	歌	歌	歌	歌					
126	市	市	市	市					
127	所	所	所	所					
128	勉	勉	勉	勉					
129	強	強	強	強					
130	有	有	有	有					
131	旅	旅	旅	旅					

第11課 2 Using Kanji

Ⅰ Write the appropriate mixes of kanji and *hiragana*.

1. 友だちから＿＿＿＿＿＿をもらいました。とても＿＿＿＿＿＿＿＿＿人です。
   　　　　　　てがみ　　　　　　　　　　　　　　　　　　あかるい

2. ＿＿＿＿＿＿を見たり、＿＿＿＿＿＿＿＿＿して、日本語を＿＿＿＿＿＿します。
   　えいが　　　　　　　　うたったり　　　　　　　　　　　べんきょう

3. 家の＿＿＿＿＿＿に＿＿＿＿＿＿があります。
   　　　ちかく　　　びょういん

4. 父は＿＿＿＿＿＿が＿＿＿＿＿＿です。
   　　　りょこう　　　すき

5. 鎌倉＿＿＿＿に住んでいます。とても＿＿＿＿＿＿な＿＿＿＿です。
   かまくら　し　　　　　　　　　　　ゆうめい　　　ところ

6. ＿＿＿＿が＿＿＿＿＿＿＿です。しょうらい、＿＿＿＿＿＿になりたいです。
   うた　　　だいすき　　　　　　　　　　　　かしゅ

Ⅱ Using the kanji you know, translate the sentences into Japanese.

1. On my days off I watch movies, sing songs, and so on.

2. My friend lives in my neighborhood.

3. Because I was sick, I did not travel.

4. Please write a letter to me.

5. I have never studied foreign languages.

第12課　1　Kanji Practice

132	昔	昔	昔	昔				
133	々	々	々	々				
134	神	神	神	神				
135	早	早	早	早				
136	起	起	起	起				
137	牛	牛	牛	牛				
138	使	使	使	使				
139	働	働	働	働				
140	連	連	連	連				
141	別	別	別	別				
142	度	度	度	度				
143	赤	赤	赤	赤				
144	青	青	青	青				
145	色	色	色	色				

第12課 2 Using Kanji

I Write the appropriate mixes of kanji and *hiragana*.

1. ＿＿＿＿＿＿＿、ある所に＿＿＿＿＿がいました。
   むかしむかし　　　　　　　　かみさま

2. ＿＿＿＿＿は＿＿＿を＿＿＿＿＿＿＿、＿＿＿＿＿＿＿いました。
   ひとびと　　　うし　　　　つかって　　　　　　はたらいて

3. 「＿＿＿＿＿は大変ですか。」「＿＿＿＿＿大変じゃないです。」
   べんきょう　　たいへん　　　　べつに　　　たいへん

4. 大人は＿＿＿＿ ＿＿＿、子どもは＿＿＿＿ ＿＿＿のＴシャツを着ています。
   おとな　あかい　いろ　　　　　　あおい　いろ　　ティー　　　き

5. ＿＿＿＿＿の休みに、友だちを＿＿＿＿＿＿ ＿＿＿＿＿＿＿。
   こんど　　　　　　　　　　つれて　　　　　かえります

6. ＿＿＿＿＿の前で、友だちと＿＿＿＿＿＿＿＿。
   じんじゃ　　　　　　　　わかれました

II Using the kanji you know, translate the sentences into Japanese.

1. I like red and blue.

2. I have been to Tokyo once.

3. I don't like getting up early in the morning.

4. I don't want to separate from you.

5. May I use a telephone?

6. I have to work on Sunday.